KU-128-479

ENGAGING TEACHERS

Towards a radical democratic
agenda for schooling

Trevor Gale and **Kathleen Densmore**

UNIVERSITY OF WALES COLLEGE NEWPORT
LIBRARY
AND
INFORMATION
SERVICES
CAERLEON

Open University Press
Maidenhead · Philadelphia

Open Universiy Press
McGraw-Hill Education
McGraw-Hill House
Shoppenhangers Road
Maidenhead
Berkshire
England
SL6 2QL

email: enquiries@openup.co.uk
world wide web: www.openup.co.uk

and
325 Chestnut Street
Philadelphia, PA 19106, USA

First Published 2003

Copyright © Trevor Gale and Kathleen Densmore, 2003

All rights reserved. Except for the quotation of short passages for the purpose
of criticism and review, no part of this publication may be reproduced, stored
in a retrieval system, or transmitted, in any form or by any means, electronic,
mechanical, photocopying, recording or otherwise, without the prior written
permission of the publisher or a licence from the Copyright Licensing Agency
Limited. Details of such licences (for reprographic reproduction) may be
obtained from the Copyright Licensing Agency Ltd of 90 Tottenham
Court Road, London, W1P 0LP.

A catalogue record of this book is available from the British Library

ISBN   0 335 21027 9 (hb)   0 335 21026 0 (pb)

Library of Congress Cataloging-in-Publication Data
Gale, Trevor, 1956–
    Engaging teachers: towards a radical democratic agenda for schooling / Trevor
Gale and Kathleen Densmore.
        p. cm.
    Includes bibliographical references and index.
    ISBN 0-335-21027-9   0-335-21026-0
    1. Critical pedagogy.   2. Privatization in education.   I. Densmore, Kathleen
Mary.   II. Title.
LC196 .G34 2003
370.11′5–dc21   2002035468

Typeset by Graphicraft Limited, Hong Kong
Printed in Great Britain by Biddles Ltd, *www.biddles.co.uk*

Contents

Foreword

Since Rousseau there has been a long and rich tradition of arguments linking education with self-determination and collective empowerment. The most important contribution is probably that of Dewey, whose *Democracy in Education* ([1916] 1966) persuaded us to locate education in the social realm, as a primary instrument in building modern democracy. The tradition of education and democracy reached a peak in the late 1960s and 1970s which saw the flourishing of activist teaching in inner-city communities in Europe, Australia and the United States. Notions gained ground of the teacher as radical professional responsible for the empowerment of all, teacher–community alliances in building community, educational leadership as collective rather than bureaucratic. These practices were deeply threatening to many in government and conservative circles, and received a battering when the new right and policies of 'market at all costs' gained ascendancy from the mid-1980s. The primary contribution made by *Engaging Teachers* is that it recovers and reconnects with the education/democracy tradition.

In doing so this book demonstrates that understanding the social context, and being at home with political and economic argument, are vital tools for democratic education. Politics and economics have for too long been used to close down democracy in schools and separate them from their local communities (who become consumers-at-a-distance). Trevor Gale and Kathleen Densmore argue that an effective understanding of politics and economics can break down the ascendancy of conservative policies and enable schools and their communities to take their future into their own hands. *Engaging Teachers* sharply illuminates the flaws in the market model of teaching and learning. The market model rests on the breathtaking claim that market economic competition is 'natural' and serves the interests of all, free political decision-making is artificial and destructive, and teachers are just a special interest group that has captured schooling for its own selfish purposes. They explain that market choice is fine if you have the material means, the private wealth, to exercise the full range of choices. It's not so good if you do not. Markets by their natural operations foster inequalities. They divide school communities, where everyone should succeed, into winners and losers. They enrich some schools and impoverish others. And in systems such as in New Zealand, the UK and parts of Australia that have reformed their government schools along market lines, markets have conspicuously failed to improve learning outcomes for students.

The key point in this argument is that capitalism and democracy are *not* natural or inevitable partners. Unfettered capitalism has no place for collective political empowerment, which forces the strong market players to become accountable to everyone, thus interfering with the 'natural mechanism' of competition. Market economics *must* be modified if every person, rich and poor, is to exercise their democratic rights in society and through education. Markets have only a limited role in formal education which above all must place high quality schooling within reach of every citizen. That was the great gain made by the politics of public education in the twentieth century. It is a gain whose achievement is incomplete – especially but not only in the developing world! – and is constantly rendered fragile by inadequate resources from government and the resort to consumerist policy and competitive allocations. But high quality universal schooling for all *is* achievable and in some countries it is done.

Engaging Teachers is written in an accessible style and an optimistic spirit. Gale and Densmore believe that human beings are neither inherently self-interested nor inherently cooperative and generous to each other. We can be either, we are what we want ourselves to be, and democratic schooling can play a great role in fashioning us as collaborative social partners. Teachers are the key players here. For the authors, teaching is politically engaged, radical, critical, collaborative, context-aware and committed to empowering everyone. In this vision, the freedom of one is the freedom of all. If these are not to be empty slogans, as they often were in the 1970s, to be realized they require long-term and substantial work. It is no small task to regenerate poor urban school communities, in which aspirations are high but educational practices have little purchase, in the context of growing inequalities on both local and global levels. And the tasks are not limited to schooling. Democracy has been undermined not just because of the strength of the market model in education policy, and the funding cutbacks in the public educational sector, but by the power of corporations and the centralization of the media and information, which enables a small number of people to set the frame for public debate. Teachers, often fine community activists, have a vital role in regenerating democracy from the bottom up. Teachers have the critical skills to unlock the myths and mystifications of much of the information that blankets our public space. They have a crucial role in building the skills of organizing and empowerment upon which self-help depends. It is no wonder that such an effort has been made to narrow the horizons of teachers and block the exercise of their broader democratic role. *Engaging Teachers* helps teachers to find a way through.

Simon Marginson
Australian Professorial Fellow
Director, Monash Centre for Research in International Education
Monash University, Australia

Acknowledgements

Even before we finished writing *Just Schooling*, the precursor to this monograph, we began to plan for *Engaging Teachers*. In our minds, there was a degree of unfinished business, things we wanted to say about both the kind of disposition we imagined for teachers committed to a radical democratic agenda for schooling and the kind of socio-cultural and economic context in which they are located. We are, therefore, grateful to Open University Press, particularly to Shona Mullen, for giving us this opportunity and for once more supporting us through the publication process. Our thanks are extended also to Simon Marginson who graciously provided the Foreword to this volume during a time of extreme work pressures. But probably most important to us are Pam and David who continue to support us through the rigours and intensity of research and writing. We are acutely aware of their contributions to this book, though these might not be readily apparent to others. In particular, we are indebted to Pam for her editing skills that helped us deliver a relatively 'clean' text to the publishers. Finally, portions of this book have appeared elsewhere in different forms and have been reworked for inclusion here. We would like to thank the publishers of the following materials: parts of Chapter 3 originally appeared in *Discourse* and a version of Chapter 4 in the *International Journal of Leadership in Education*.

one

Introduction: to a politics of engagement

A colleague recently relayed to one of us his experience of a corporate teambuilding exercise organized for the support staff of a university department: a few days away at a resort at the university's expense, facilitated by a zealous workshop consultant. The retreat took its theme from the following story:

> A man was walking along the beach one morning, enjoying the warmth of the early morning sun, the fresh breeze and the solitude. In the distance he noticed another man repeatedly bending over, picking something up from the water's edge and throwing it into the sea. As the first man approached the second, he could see that the beach was littered with starfish, washed up by the waves. 'What are you doing?' he inquired, as he came within hearing. 'I'm giving them another chance at life', the man replied. 'But there are thousands of them. You could be at it all day and still not make a difference.' The second man bent down one more time, picked up another starfish and threw it into the ocean. 'It made a difference for that one', he remarked.

In keeping with the theme of the retreat, each participant received a small badge in the shape of a starfish, to remind them of the moral of the story, that every member of the organization can make a difference, irrespective of their position and irrespective of the enormity of the problems they might face – including the scepticism and inaction of others. One staff member was particularly moved and motivated by the experience and upon her return to work continued to wear her badge and retell the story to all who inquired. At the end of one retelling in the staffroom one morning, a colleague who was a marine biologist in the department responded: 'But they were dead anyway. That's why they were washed up on the beach.'

We retell this story at the outset, not to imply that everyday people cannot make a difference to their own and others' circumstances and life prospects. On the contrary, we believe that people *can* make a difference to their futures and to the futures of their communities. Our point, however, is that not everything we do will or can make a difference, particularly when our actions are ill-informed and/or naïve about the wider contexts in which we operate. For instance, some teachers continue to believe that all that students need do to 'get ahead', even students located in disadvantaged communities, is to combine their abilities with effort and persistence. Many teachers put in long hours working with students convinced of the truth of this premise, efforts that are reinforced by the occasional success story or the hope of one. Others are more cynical, convinced that schools predominantly play a reproductive role in society rather than a reconstructive one or they feel that as teachers they cannot do much anyway given the disadvantages students bring with them to the classroom. Still other teachers feel guilty for failing to meet the high expectations they hold for themselves.

Given the assault of the New Right on education and its subsequent reconfiguration within society during the 1980s and 1990s, many teachers have found themselves faced with such choices: whether to continue to believe in an education system that offers hope for a better future or whether to face the prospect that only some benefit from education and that these beneficiaries are more identifiable by their socio-economic status than their comparative ability and effort. Of course, these are extreme positions and few teachers are reduced to such choices, even though these may be what others expect of them. Generally, teachers are more intellectually and politically resourceful than these positions imply and are able to discern alternatives not envisaged by others. Nevertheless, we are concerned that several of these alternatives, as taken up by teachers, approximate the extremes of acquiescence, withdrawal and anxiety, which threaten to undermine their competence and their students' futures.

In addressing these matters, *Engaging Teachers* makes a deliberate attempt to reclaim the education discourse captured by New Right politics and to connect it with a radical democratic agenda for schooling. On its agenda are education markets, policy, leadership, professionalism and communities. Their engagement in this book is conceived on at least two levels. First, as encouragement for teachers to become and/or to continue to be involved in reconstructing schooling for socially just purposes and in democratic ways. From this perspective, the politics of engagement is not a matter of giving in or simply fighting back but is informed by a commitment to generate alternatives. We are particularly concerned with alternatives that offer the possibility of transforming both schools and society in radical democratic directions. This is because we believe that public schools and society currently place serious limits on the ability and opportunity for teachers, students, parents and other community members to work together to make things happen, rather than to have things done to them (Giddens 1994). Thus, our intent is to provocatively argue the importance of a commitment to work collectively in order to explore and act on common interests, across uncommon ground.

Second, the book conceives of teachers engaging in these reconstructive efforts in attractive and meaningful ways, as distinct from exchanges conceived within education markets. For us, the attraction is decisions about schooling made by those these decisions affect and decisions that are meaningful because they engage the interests of all. These two foci are inherently interconnected: we hope to contribute to making both public schooling and society more democratic; by working on one we also understand our efforts as contributing to the other. We begin by outlining what we mean by a politics of engagement: its conception of democratic participation, its political and theoretical disposition and its commitment to informed action. This is followed by an overview of the book's content, not just an account of what can be found in the following chapters but also the arguments that inform and connect them. In brief, we draw attention to four main themes that pervade *Engaging Teachers*, namely:

- the influence of the market in education, its anti-democratic agenda, and the need for teachers to think and act differently if the individual and collective futures of all students are to be rescued;
- the continued although changed influence of government and institutions in the education marketplace, characterized by increased control at the same time as reduced responsibility;
- the need for teachers to be cognizant of the 'big picture' informing education, to engage with it and to connect this with local community action, and
- the need for teachers and schools to more fully engage with their communities in radical democratic ways.

Engagement as political commitment and activism

A central issue, then, in this book – which runs through each of these four themes – involves teachers' *engagement* with schooling and with the broader social, political and economic conditions within which this is framed. As we argue throughout, these conditions are currently dominated by a market discourse that signals a point of departure for teachers committed to recognitive justice (Gale and Densmore 2000). From our perspective, critical engagement with this market discourse is informed by three interrelated and overlapping concepts: radical democracy, a socially critical disposition and political activism. We introduce each of these in turn.

Radical democracy

Sitting on committees is not necessarily democratic, irrespective of the outcomes these committees might achieve. Committees might represent structures of democracy (forums in which democratic agendas can be pursued), they might be representative of a broad range of interests, and they might even make decisions that benefit many people. But if they are structures 'designed to empower the people, not the people empowered' (Lummis 1996: 23), then they have little claim on democracy. In short, it is the politics that names and frames committee work and committee members, which determine its (democratic) character. What can be done inside committees is constrained and enabled by this politics and what goes on outside committees is frequently just as important as what goes on inside them. Public and private institutions in western countries are full of examples of committees that are not democratic, even at the same time as there are those that are. Schools and education systems are no different in this regard. What happens within schools and what happens outside them are important in understanding their contribution to the democratization of society. Some teachers, students and parents are empowered by their experiences of school and the opportunities that schools present, but not all; hence Connell's observation that 'democratization *in* the school is not necessarily the same as democratization *of* the school' (Connell 1993: 71, original emphasis).

What, then, do we mean by democracy and, particularly, what do we mean by radical democracy? First, while we agree that democracy 'describes an ideal, not a method for achieving it' (Lummis 1996: 22), this is not to say that the ways in which we achieve things are outside the purview of democracy. That is, as far as democracy is concerned, the ends do not justify the means. Indeed, democratizing processes and practices, whether in committees or in classrooms, is central to what it means to pursue democracy: the people empowered. This is so because power is not so much a thing that can be held as it is a thing that is exercised. We see power predominantly when it is in action; we might see the effects of power – material and social benefits and rewards, and the absence of these – but they are not the same as acts of power. Even those who hold great wealth, position, status and so on, are not powerful without mobilizing their resources or there is the threat and/or possibility for their mobilization. It is this understanding of democracy as a form of power, that causes Lummis to remark: 'If the word means what it says, there is democracy where the people have the power . . . It is because there is no sure, fixed solution to this puzzle – the puzzle of how to realize democracy in our collective life – that our commitment to it can take the form only of a historical project' (Lummis 1996: 22). By definition, an historical project is ongoing and necessarily includes processes, actions and practices. Yet, such projects extend over time and are never complete. To repeat, democracy is an ideal; it guides what we do and how we do it, even though these in the end are approximations and hence themselves incomplete.

Second, it is these approximations or, more often, modifications that capture the attention and imagination of democrats in many so-called democratic societies; democrats who are concerned about democracy's subversion by those who lay their own claims on power:

> 'Democracy' was once a word of the people, a critical word, a revolutionary word. It has been stolen by those who would rule over the people, to add legitimacy to their rule. It is time to take it back, to restore to it its critical and radical power . . . This is a call, then, for a

rectification of names. That means insisting that the word 'democracy' be used only to describe democratic things.

(Lummis 1996: 15)

As even a casual reading of *Engaging Teachers* will reveal, we think these are pertinent comments with regard to the marketization of just about everything in contemporary western nations and the particular threat this poses to a democratic education. However, proponents of markets are not without their own accounts of democracy, which are usually expressed in terms of individual freedoms (see Chapters 2 and 6). This 'muddying of the waters' poses a similar threat to democracy and is one of the main reasons we give so much of our attention in this book to naming the anti-democratic agendas of markets, as well as those of governments and institutions. On their conflicting claims to democracy, Lummis comments: 'In answer to the question "Which kind of democracy are you talking about?" it would be best if we could say, "Not any of the modified democracies – the thing itself." Just democracy, which is self-defining: the people's having the power' (1996: 24).

It is worth considering Lummis' reference here to 'people's'. In our view, deleting the apostrophe would deliver a much richer account of radical democracy.[1] This new reading of people*s* would signal an explicit recognition of difference *and* similarity; an understanding of groups with internal cultural likenesses relating with other groups from whom they might differ, yet all with the potential for working together. In short, as much as people have shared experiences, radical democracy should also recognize and value their differences. *Just* democracy indeed! In our view, society is not comprised of atomistic individuals but social classes, racial/ethnic and gender groups with specific interests. Ultimately, if we take seriously a commitment to educate *all* children, society must be democratized so that all peoples have meaningful voices in the running of all facets of their lives (see, for example, Lauder and Wylie 1990).

This also serves as introduction to 'the thing itself'. While Lummis' preference is not to modify democracy (with 'liberal', 'social', 'popular', 'strong', 'market' and so on), he cedes to using 'radical' in order to distinguish it from other accounts of democracy and to express solidarity with those who in the past and in the present have called themselves 'radical democrats'. There are good reasons for adopting radical as a modifier for democracy, first because it is not a true modifier in the sense of adapting or moderating, but an intensifier: 'Radical democracy means democracy in its essential form, democracy at its root, quite precisely the thing itself' (Lummis 1996: 25). Second, the word 'radical' draws attention to the political character of democracy and distinguishes it from other more dominating forms of power: 'Democracy *is* politically radical' (Lummis 1996: 25, original emphasis). To advocate a politics that is not simply intent on empowering people but is identified by 'the people empowered', is distinctly different from many power relations in contemporary societies. Third, 'radical' suggests motion,

'not lateral to the edge (as with "left") but straight down to the source
... the vital source of energy at the centre of all living politics' (Lummis
1996: 25).

It is this dynamic and the centrality of democracy – of people themselves
empowered – that we take as a defining character for engaging teachers. In
our view, such teachers:

- believe it is possible for ordinary people to have real decision-making
  authority over those things that most affect them;
- assume the obligation of transforming everyday practices so that the norms
  and symbols that ordinarily go unquestioned are analysed and changed in
  ways that no longer oppress others;
- simultaneously enhance the individual and advance the community;
- exercise and develop their creative and problem-solving capacities by
  participating in the lives of communities, and
- help others and let themselves become transformed through their participation in common work.

Notwithstanding important political and philosophical differences over
whether or not democracy is a univocal concept, our modest orientation
in *Engaging Teachers* presupposes that progress can be made in democracy
and that major advances in democracy can and must be protected. By
engaging others and ourselves in democratic practices we also learn about
the advantages of such practices. This is so for students, parents and community members as much as it is for teachers.

A socially critical disposition

As with the reference to *radical* democracy – signalling a specific kind of
democratic polity and, therefore, a specific form of engagement – to suggest
that teachers' engagement with schooling and society should be *critical* is
also to set it apart as overtly political (Carspecken 1996: 2). Having a socially critical disposition involves a similar kind of politics, which is not as
simple as criticizing what we do not like or what is not working, although
this is not excluded. For example, we are not enthusiastic about markets
infiltrating and dictating to contemporary social relations and it would be
fair to say that we expend considerable effort in the following chapters in
criticizing them. We particularly do not like the prospect of public schools
looking like whatever the market says they should look like. This is because
we are committed to the idea of schooling making a difference, especially
for students who have been historically mis- and underserved by public
education. And we do not see markets contributing very much to this
making-a-difference agenda; anything but! In fact, we are concerned that
the market is continuing and deepening this disservice to students at the
same time as it is undermining past and present efforts to redress social
and educational inequalities. But our engagement with these issues is also

positive; while our critique is of the negative influences of the market, it also includes positive suggestions and recommendations about how things might be different.

These are not thoughts and commitments that are ours alone. It is clear that there is some variation among social scientists about what it means to be 'critical'; some are neo-Marxist in orientation, for example, while others are post-structural and/or postmodern. However, those of us with a socially critical disposition 'are all concerned about social inequalities, and we direct our work toward positive social change' (Carspecken 1996: 3). These two political interests, then, define what it means to be critically engaged: (1) to seek to identify what is *really* going on, particularly who benefits and who does not by current social arrangements (including the arrangements of schooling but also within society more generally); and (2) to articulate what can be done about these. Agger probably states this more forcefully, particularly in relation to schooling:

> ... the critical sociology of education, much of which has migrated to the United States from the UK and Australia, is concerned not only to identify domination (e.g., Bowles and Gintis's (1976) classic work on what they call 'the hidden curriculum') but also to identify and foster 'resistances' both in the classroom and curriculum and in the ways educational administrators run their institutions.
>
> (Agger 1998: 175–6)

As implied by Agger, a basic assumption of socially critical work and workers is 'that certain groups in any society are privileged over others ... [and this is at the heart of] the oppression which characterizes contemporary societies' (Kincheloe and McLaren 1994: 140). In this regard, Carspecken perhaps best summarizes our own critical disposition:

> ... we criticalists [Carspecken's term for those who share a socially critical disposition] have both witnessed and directly experienced forms of oppression. We do not like them. We want to change them. The precise nature of oppression, however, is an empirical question and not a given belief. Much of our research attempts to clarify how and where oppression works.
>
> (1996: 8)

As already noted, the particular forms of oppression addressed in this book are those that currently dominate the economies of western nations and which tend to render social relations subservient to markets. The principal academic discipline upon which we draw to conduct this critique is critical sociology but we also engage in a 'radical political economy' (Sayer 1995) of education:[2] 'Radical political economy is of course a *critical* social science, both explaining and criticizing the practices it studies, with the explicit aim of reducing illusion and freeing people from domination and unwanted forces' (Sayer 1995: 7, original emphasis). By way of comparison, these are:

... approaches which view the economy as socially and politically embedded and as structured by power relations ... [Moreover] political economy is often counterposed to a more right-wing 'economics' or 'liberal economics', in which economic affairs are treated ahistorically and as largely separable from political and social affairs.

(Sayer 1995: ix)

For now, we leave discussion of such comparisons and separations to the following chapters. Here it is enough to note that teachers who employ a socially critical disposition:

- engage in the production of knowledge, at global as well as local levels;
- enable teachers and students to analyse their location within an increasingly stratified society;
- help others identify and act upon the injustices that have historically been imposed upon people throughout the world, and
- maintain social justice ideals, ensuring that resources and opportunities go first to those most in need and that school processes are cognizant of and responsive to cultural differences.

Finally, critical social science has a disposition for dialectic relations. This means that critically engaged teachers are prepared to live with uncertainty and ambiguity, not that they are necessarily happy with these but willing nevertheless to embrace them. With others and in front of students and parents they reflect upon and grapple with changing circumstances to which there may be no perfectly satisfactory answers. This dialectic is in keeping with how Pierre Bourdieu (Bourdieu and Wacquant 1992) envisages 'habitus' and which he sometimes explains as disposition: a concept he appropriated and developed to embody the apparent competing interests and possibilities of structure and agency, which inform our actions.

Political activism

Individual and group commitment to taking action in difficult circumstances provides a third dimension to engagement. Such political activism is related to: (1) radical democracy's comparison to motion and 'the vital source of energy at the centre of all living politics' (Lummis 1996: 25); as well as to (2) critical social science and its commitment to articulate what can be done about the injustices it uncovers. These relationships also suggest that the activism of teacher engagement is of a particular form: overtly political in nature and emanicipatory in kind. In this regard, Deem *et al.*, writing on 'active citizenship', make the distinction between:

... an individual model favoured by the Right and a social model preferred by the Left. At the centre of the individual model lies charity, through which individuals reach out to others and thereby become citizens through philanthropic action. In the social model, it is the community that acts to provide the conditions for citizenship and citizenship is attained through political involvement.

(Deem et al. 1995: 48–9)

It is this second form of activism that we wish to investigate in our account of *Engaging Teachers*. This is not to discount the value of individuals giving from their wealth to other individuals who are in need, but to argue that political activism, informed by radical democracy and a socially critical disposition, necessarily involves a collective political dimension. As we argue in Chapter 2, individuals exist in relation; their actions need to be similarly motivated. The individualism of neoliberal markets, then:

> ... is an argument against state action and in favour of self-help which . . . 'releases people from a welfare culture'. [Whereas] The notion of a regenerated civil society filled with voluntary associations composed of enterprising participants, resonates to some extent with the notions of citizenship and citizen empowerment preferred by the Left.
>
> (Deem et al. 1995: 48)

The extent to which this resonates with how we understand teachers' engagement in schools and with students and their communities, is limited by the implication that governments and other broad collectives have a minimal role to play in agitating against social and economic inequalities and injustices. Clearly, we do not believe this to be the case. Political activism is needed within and by government, across nations, as much as it needs to be engaged by individuals working with others within communities and across nations. Nevertheless, we do see value in notions of 'generative politics' which 'allow individuals and groups to make things happen, rather than have things happen to them' (Giddens 1994: 15). This is not to put the burden of activism on the shoulders of teachers alone. While they are indispensable agents of educational change (Fullan and Hargreaves 1996), organizing people school by school and community by community is also essential for discussion, debate and problem solving. What this will look like in form and content will vary depending upon each community. Our point is that ground needs to be laid through persistent involvement in the midst of local politics, over time. Alliances among people based on divergent, as well as converging, interests need to be formed. At the same time, 'interests' need to be scrutinized, identifying and articulating diverse values and standpoints. The challenge is to learn to think and help others think more in terms of 'us' and less in terms of 'me'. Indeed, it might now be possible to (re)construct a notion of objective interests.

This also leads us to think about the place for teachers' political activism within larger forums. In recognizing that many of the most serious problems confronting teachers and school administrators have their origins in broader socio-economic and historical contexts, *Engaging Teachers* refrains from simply exhorting the people who work in schools to work harder and smarter. But hierarchies of subordination and the inequality of power and control over resources and opportunities in society suggest that unless teachers engage with broader political projects, their efforts inside schools alone will not produce the benefits they seek. For example, at the beginning of the twenty-first century some school district officials in New York maintain that the market is signalling that public education need only be mandatory through to Grade 8. They argue that those people who want more education can pay for it themselves.

This argument about what the economy 'needs' can be taken more or less strongly. In its strongest sense, the economy is a functionally closed system. However, there are other ways in which to engage with arguments about who decides what the economy and students need by way of an education. In particular, we believe that everyday people have the capability to collectively decide how to realize their own human potential. The Algebra Project (Moses *et al.* 2001) in the United States provides one way to think about this. This national mathematics literacy campaign aims at engaging low-income students and students of colour to create a demand for the skills and understandings required in order to complete algebra by the eighth grade and be positioned to access a college preparatory mathematics sequence in high school. The curriculum draws on students' experiences to lead them to an understanding of algebraic concepts. The project takes a geographically regional approach throughout the southern United States and includes community development, youth leadership development and teacher development. Youth of colour become peer-leaders and cultural catalysts to help build networks of mathematically literate youth. The project thus creates a demand within low-income and minority communities for education.

Irrespective of its grand scale, this is still political activism and demonstrates what can be done when space is available for groups of people to take collective action on projects that directly affect them. As Yeatman notes:

> Activism is a category of political action which is wed to the participatory conceptions of democracy that have come to displace paternalistic models of democracy in the last several decades. Paternalistic models of democracy are those that cast the vast majority of the subjects of democratic government in whatever jurisdiction is considered (nation, organization or school) as those in whose interests a professional elite of some kind rules.
>
> (1998a: 32)

As we argue in this book, we think this paternal democracy and its ruling professional elite have been or are in the process of being usurped by a market democracy and a corporate elite, which have cut the paternal 'apron strings' so to speak. We are also more wedded to a radical democracy as its alternative, given our arguments above, although we recognize Yeatman's conception of participatory democracy as having similar sentiments. Notwithstanding these realignments, we agree with Yeatman about the place for activism – in all jurisdictions, big and small – and the potential for its engagement by all peoples. In our view, then, teacher activists are those that:

- agitate for greater educational funding and more redistributive expenditure;
- engage in attempts to reverse or end cycles of inequalities, arrested opportunities and injustices;
- think more in terms of 'us' and less in terms of 'me', and
- assume the need to work closely with others to bring about lasting change.

To be an activist is to be centrally involved, to be a player; playing in such a way as to change 'the immanent rules of the game' (Bourdieu and Wacquant 1992: 99). In this role, teacher activists are engaged in posing different and alternative futures from the conventional wisdom of schooling and society. Teachers' engagement in public forums is also an important tactic in redressing New Right efforts to locate all social problems within the school (see Chapter 6). That is, where the politics is played out can often dictate the nature of the politics (see Chapter 3). Finally, Yeatman observes in her research that political activists (in policy contexts) 'were people highly motivated by some conception of social justice and who sought to make a difference' (1998a: 1). This is what we hope for in *Engaging Teachers*, particularly for a political activism motivated by recognitive notions of social justice in schooling (Gale and Densmore 2000). As Dewey suggests, our 'chief business' as educators is to enable people to 'share in a common life' (1966: 7). Teachers' political activism is about such enabling.

Organization and content issues

As noted above, the chapters following this one focus on education markets, policy, leadership, professionalism, and communities. There is a sense in which each sets the scene for those that follow but it is equally possible for readers to move back and forth between chapters according to their needs and interests. At the very least we hope that readers will want to revisit parts they have found particularly helpful and to make internal comparisons to allow some parts of the book to inform their understandings of others. Most chapters begin with *Guiding Questions/Issues* and end with *Questions for Discussion/Research* and *Suggested Readings*. The questions for discussion/ research are provided for readers as a way of stimulating and extending discussion and/or further research in relation to the issues raised in each chapter. Whether utilized for discussion or research, the questions should be seen as starting points from which other questions may be added or developed. By including such questioning in relation to our work, we hope to create spaces for its critique, not just reinforcement of our own ideas. The suggested readings are for those seeking further insight into the issues raised in each chapter. Some engage with specific issues in greater depth and/or add to the overall discussion, while others question and, at some points, provide quite different accounts of these issues. It should be noted that the lists are far from exhaustive. Other possible sources can be found in the reference section.

Along with our political and theoretical orientations outlined above, the arguments we mount are informed by our engagement with the relevant academic literature, our knowledge and experiences of education in contemporary western societies and our reading of the broader socio-economic conditions it confronts. In this account, data utilized in our work tends to be illustrative rather than formative of these arguments and are derived from a larger corpus of data and research we have conducted, which is broadly concerned with detailing a political and cultural economy of education, particularly in relation to democratic and socially just practices in education. As the following chapters illustrate, the cluster of research projects on which this book draws sustains a range of foci but all are concerned with the various ways in which educators engage with the marketization of education at levels of practice.

Chapter 3, for example, draws on data from a case study of an Australian high school and is focused on teachers', parents' and students' engagement with schooling, the tactics they employ in reworking this to suit their own values and circumstances, and the 'space' available for them to do so. The specific data utilized in that chapter relate to teachers' responses to standardized testing policy, as understood by the school's principal. Discussions in Chapter 4 are informed by research into the production of Australian higher education entry policy, particularly theories of how political activists establish and negotiate spaces for action, as these apply to issues of educational leadership. As with Chapter 3, Chapter 5 contains considerable direct citation of data, in this case taken from research focused on student–teachers', teachers' and teacher–educators' understandings of their professionalism. In Chapters 2 and 6, direct evidence of our data is less prolific but nonetheless drawn from fieldwork and scholarship concerned with the extent to which getting a 'good' education is seen as a public matter and/or a private one. All of the data we utilize are in the form of semi-structured interviews. Reference to them includes an indication of the location and positioning from which interviewees speak: their vocality. In Chapter 5, this referencing system is more elaborate given the number and diversity of the interviewees it cites.

Throughout these chapters, a major theme, perhaps *the* major theme, concerns the marketization of education. This is explicitly addressed in Chapter 2 but also in subsequent chapters, particularly Chapters 4 and 6. This level of attention reflects the fact that we regard it to be one of the most potent influences in contemporary western societies, pervading almost all aspects of what it now means to get an education and what it now means to deliver it. In engaging with these issues we examine what we consider to be the three claimed virtues of markets:

- the *absence of a central controlling influence* (such as government), given the investment of authority in dispersed consumers, thereby making it truly democratic; a virtue referred to as the free or invisible hand of the market;

- the *empowering of individuals*, given their freedom to choose rather than being forced to accept the limitations, in particular, of a controlling government; engendering virtues of individual fairness, natural justice and the depoliticization of everyday life, and
- the *recognition of individuals as consumers* (rather than productive workers in a neo-Marxist sense) whose actions are largely governed by self-interest (which justifies the application of market logic to almost all aspects of social and economic life); largely a vice counterbalanced by the virtue of individuals' philanthropic actions.

In *Engaging Teachers* we take issue with these claims – which constitute significant reworking of the commitments we outline above – particularly in relation to education but also in the context of social relations more broadly. We also point out ways in which these claims work to demonize collectives and their representatives, including government and practically anything public. All three are dealt with at some length in subsequent chapters but we wish to linger here for a moment to focus on the problematic of the freedom of choice, given its centrality to the internal logic of markets. The point we wish to reinforce is that choice is rarely free and unrestricted; in fact, it is frequently highly restricted. We are not arguing here against agency but we do want to acknowledge structure, to retain a sense of our habitus.

The ability to choose a product, once a consumer has made the decision to do so, is dogged by constraint. *Opportunity*, or the lack of it, presents itself as a first hurdle. We may wish to purchase a particular product, for example, but it might be out of stock, in stock but located elsewhere and unreachable, still in production, or simply not yet invented or committed to being produced. A motor vehicle that utilizes absolutely no fossil fuels might be one example; a school in our district equipped with the latest electronic information technologies might be another. Choices, as this first condition implies, are also constrained by (the lack of) *information* about available goods and services. For example, the main telephone company in Australia, one of the world's most profitable, is required by law to provide a free dial-up directory service, which it does. In fact, it runs two such services. However, the second – the one that it advertises to potential consumers – incurs a service charge. Limits on *knowledge* and *understanding* similarly restrict choice. Buying a video recorder or a mobile phone on a 'plan' that includes calls is a good example. It is not simply a matter of selecting on the basis of quality and cost. Similarly priced products can come with an array of features and services, which almost seem designed to trap the naïve and/or novice. In such circumstances, Henry Ford's quip that 'You can have any colour as long as it's black' (Simper 1994: 47) appears almost comforting.

Cost is an obvious restriction on choice; some simply cannot afford some products (without 'equity scholarships' to attend university, for example), can only afford them at low prices and quality (such as the state's provision of 'safety net' schooling) or are duped into paying more for what they believe to be the price for quality (fees for private schools of marginal benefit, for instance). Hence, the *exchange value* of goods and services is a better indicator than cost, of the restrictions on choice. For example, many marginalized black people potentially give up a lot more than their white middle-class counterparts when they acquire a white middle-class education. The relative costs can be high while the returns few, and vice versa. This raises the issue of *profit*. As we have implied, consumers are less likely than producers to profit from their choices. And if freedom of choice in the market is seen to be a fallacy, self-interest and dispersed governance also face potential collapse. Without real freedom to choose, it hardly can be argued that one's self-interests have been fulfilled. Indeed, the interests that appear to be most served by the above exchanges are those of producers, a formidable collective in the marketplace that may exhibit some internal squabbles but overall wields incredible control over consumers. (See Chapter 3 for a discussion of producer/consumer relations in the context of education policy.)

Chapter 2 illustrates the above argumentation, namely the influence of the market, its anti-democratic agenda and the need for teachers to think and act differently. Educators are aware of much of what we say in that chapter but in a general sense. Like most people, educators spend their time learning about other things. This is one reason why many do not necessarily see how patterns of global economic restructuring might influence what they do in their daily (working) lives. Yet changing our environment requires a good grasp of what schools do and why they do it. According to the New Right, a central problem with 'big' government, or the Welfare State, is that the 'consumer' has little say in how social services, such as schools, should be run. This, the argument goes, is largely because the professionals who work in these sectors have too much control over what and how services or goods are provided. Such a view of teachers is addressed in Chapters 2, 5 and 6. Together, these chapters point to how neoliberal reforms and ideology have resulted in scarce opportunities in many schools for teachers to genuinely participate in democratic decision-making of all possible types, at all possible levels. We believe this view also reduces teachers' status in society, dissuades others from entering the field and contributes to low morale among teachers.

Chapter 3 shows the continued, although changed, influence of government in education, characterized by the seemingly unlikely combination of increased control and reduced responsibility. Here we show how the policy process in education reinforces the managerial perspective discussed in Chapter 2. Educational policy, as an instrument of management, can be viewed as an attempt to regulate which interests are excluded or silenced and which are included and heard. While the impact of any particular policy always remains an empirical question, Chapter 3 argues for viewing the policy process as one of legitimating 'who' gets to make policy and 'how', in contexts with real constraints (particularly for teachers) and real possibilities. Regarding the latter, we argue that teachers approximate policy producers (rather than policy consumers) when they put policy to use in ways different from those intended and/or when they subvert the intent of policy when it is not what they intend.

Similarly, Chapters 4 and 5 argue that there is an urgent need for teachers and schools to more fully engage with their communities in radical democratic ways. For many of us, this will be a new endeavour. Chapter 4 in particular offers an approach to school leadership that is democratic. While democratic leadership runs against the grain of current market impulses, we suggest that there is the need and the right of all those involved in the educational process to be substantively and critically involved in determining the substance, form and management of that process. With this in mind, we outline enabling strategies and tactics for leaders in education to engage. Then, because of potential conflicts between professional and community interests – harnessed by the New Right to undermine bureaucratic control – Chapter 5 examines teacher professionalism and suggests different ways that teachers might think of their roles and responsibilities. For example, we argue that the more teachers know about their communities' histories and environments, the more likely they will want to experiment with increasingly sophisticated ways to use that knowledge in their pedagogy. In a similar vein, Chapter 6 argues for the need for teachers to be cognizant of the big picture, to engage with it – not to think it is beyond them – and to connect this with local community action. This is not to suggest that the current economic and political situation should dictate what our worldview should be. Indeed, in Chapter 6 we hope we have, at a minimum, called into question the assumption that an economic perspective, and a narrow one at that, affords the most sophisticated worldview in the twenty-first century. Concerns for equity, social justice, democracy and the common good are, for us, at least as important.

Conclusion

In summary, *Engaging Teachers* aims to counter the tendency to seek simple solutions to complex problems. Our premise is that schools, and the teaching and learning that goes on inside them, must be understood within the context of the patterns of global economic restructuring. While commonly observed to have emerged since the late 1970s, this restructuring has in fact been going on for a very long time, albeit not in exactly the same ways in all countries. Precisely because these changes have been occurring over time, it can be difficult to discern the profound effect they are having in general as well as in specific communities and schools. For this reason, *Engaging Teachers* highlights what we consider to be the consequences of neoliberal policies for public education and school–community relations. We argue that to adhere to these policies is to ignore key issues concerning the material conditions needed for educational success and the prescriptions we are being asked to swallow: the supposed virtues of extreme individualism. Along with Ball (1999), we worry that adherence to the common principles underlying these policies encourages the development of pedagogic technicians rather than engaged teachers.

With *Engaging Teachers* we also hope that we have contributed, even if only in a small way, to the body of critical scholarship that recognizes the importance for all of us to have a working understanding of politics and economics. Without such an understanding, the links among social disadvantage, social justice, democracy and education are less clear and, therefore, less available to us. However, with an informed disposition together with a commitment to engage with others, especially with those who are oppressed or marginalized, radical transformations towards democracy are possible. Our view of human nature is that human beings are neither inherently self-serving nor inherently cooperative; rather, these are qualities that can be encouraged by circumstances. Hence, the meaning we assign to *engagement* recognizes the real possibility that if we can understand which conditions nurture cooperation, creativity and truly equal opportunities for developing our uniquely human capabilities and which conditions constrain their development, we can accelerate movement towards a radical democratic society.

Questions for discussion/research

- Which values underpin the assumption that capitalism and democracy are inseparable?
- What are the implications of deferring to the market for notions of social justice and democracy?
- What conflicts occur between education that has, as its purpose, furthering the common good and an education that aims to provide maximum benefits to individuals?
- In what ways can teachers engage with these issues in the context of their schools and communities?

Suggested readings

Ball, S. (1999) *Global Trends in Educational Reform and the Struggle for the Soul of the Teacher*. London: Centre for Public Policy Research, King's College.

Barber, B. (1984) *Strong Democracy, Participatory Politics for a New Age*. Berkeley, CA: University of California Press, Chapter 6.

Cunningham, F. (1987) *Democratic Theory and Socialism*. Cambridge: Cambridge University Press, Chapters 3 and 4.

Grimmett, P. and Neufeld, J. (eds) (1994) *Teacher Development and the Struggle for Authenticity: Professional Growth and Restructuring in the Context of Change*. New York: Teachers College Press, Chapter 7.

Markets: an increasingly visible hand

Conflicting ideas and values about the nature and purpose of education lie at the heart of current debates over education in contemporary societies. Economic and political trends both generate and influence these conflicts, manifested in the contested meanings currently given to democracy. In many western nations, a 'market democracy' (Chubb and Moe 1990) is promoted as the best hope for dismantling unresponsive bureaucracies – including government-directed attempts at distributing and redistributing resources and services – on the pretext that markets enable individuals to exercise their (democratic) freedom of choice as consumers. In this account, unregulated markets are held as necessary for the development of a democratic society while virtue is seen to be vested in the 'invisible hand' of the market. Invisibility in this sense means that power and control are (purportedly) spread throughout the market in the actions of atomized consumers who are represented as having the ultimate power to buy and sell goods and services at will, including their education. This market version of 'people power' is glorified as the superior means for creating wealth, a wealth that benefits all. Its glorification resides not only in an often-touted efficiency and effectiveness of markets but also in its moral virtue. There is (to be) no controlling bureaucracy engineering the decentralization or centralization of industries or services. Rather, free, invisible market forces (are able to) 'naturally' sort out successes from failures in social and economic relations.

Guiding questions/issues

In our view, however, the hand of the market has become increasingly visible; that is, some hands more than others seem to hold the levers of control managing the affairs of economy, society and environment. The benefits of a market democracy appear to be increasingly invested in an elite few, to the detriment of many. What all this means for education and educators is the focus of this chapter. In particular, we ask:

- Is market competition a model for ensuring that all students receive quality education?
- What precisely is the link between economy, education and democracy?
- Does democracy require social and economic equality?
- Can 'social' rather than 'individual' rights strengthen individual freedom?

The better we understand the scope of political and economic forces and relations, and their connections, the better we will comprehend the alternative agendas of competing perspectives and the better we can evaluate, modify and propose alternative measures for educational reform. It is for this reason that the first three sections of this chapter are devoted to outlining the economic restructuring and shift in thinking that have occurred throughout the western world – most easily observable since the late 1970s – towards the 'New Right'. Elements of this shift include different types of state intervention in the economy and the currently popular focus on individuals: their autonomy, their choices and their wealth creation. We also consider the implications of some of the contradictions inherent in this reformation. Following this overview of capitalist markets in contemporary western nations, we turn to the marketization of education and what this means for achieving a more socially just and democratic society. The above questions guide these discussions and should be kept in mind throughout. As a whole, the chapter also sets the scene for the chapters that follow, its themes particularly taken up in Chapters 4 and 6 in the contexts of educational leadership with community and school relations.

Putting the public interest out to tender

Scholars studying western industrialized countries have noted striking similarities among contemporary educational reforms that reject the social-democratic principles underlying mid-twentieth-century government interventions in the economy; namely, a strong public sector, market regulation and fiscal control over growth. Broadly, reforms to these levers of control are viewed as both indicative of the dismantling of the welfare state and as informed by ideology of the 'New Right'. This resurgent political and economic stance refers to a range of views that, in some ways, are contradictory and include both conservative social values and neoliberal economic theories – themselves not monolithic. One example of these contradictions is that many social conservatives seek to centralize control over schools, tying schooling more directly to upholding traditional values in learning and teaching, in social relations and even in doing business. On the other hand, neoliberals look more to the private sector and its competitive disposition to solve educational and economic problems.

This conjoining of neoconservative and neoliberal ideas has been taken up in different ways in different western nations, depending upon their specific political and economic circumstances (Dale and Ozga 1993). It is, therefore, only in very general terms that we can claim a similar reappraisal, across nations and regions, of guiding principles for economics and governance and which constitute the New Right. That said, market incentives are now generally seen to motivate both individuals and institutions to exercise initiative and to create and sell their products to an ever-expanding sea of self-interested consumers. Similarly, individual consumers now have greater freedom to choose among multiple producers and products, largely unrestricted by their geography. Such changes in the order of things have also frustrated democratic politics, particularly in providing for those seen to be without initiative, creativity and the wealth to consume. This is because government attempts to provide even minimal support or opportunities, including support for the poor and ethnic minorities, are increasingly viewed as an exacerbation of social and economic problems, not a solution. Instead, in market terms, an ideal social order is premised upon free choice and consumer rights while the goal of self-development is competitive, to create personal wealth.

The subsequent debate over whether or not, to what extent and in which areas the government should influence the outcomes and operations of the market, can be seen in the following historical sketch. With the crisis of the worldwide Depression in 1929, the market economies of industrial countries stagnated and the world market nearly collapsed. No country was left untouched. The crisis also created a potential for severe social unrest. It became necessary for governments to stimulate their economies and introduce new institutions in order to foster economic stability. For example, massive public works programs attempted to put the unemployed back into productive work. The solution was Keynesian (named after the economic principles espoused by John Keynes), and prompted an opening up of the functionings of government to include direct intervention in all aspects of the economic process – industry, housing, banking, infrastructure and so on – financed on the basis of anticipated future economic growth. To be a major investor in the economy had never before been considered part of the state's role. Nevertheless, beginning in the 1930s, this strong government involvement in providing citizens with social support and societies with economic direction continued through much of the twentieth century. It was an explicit role for government that was both political and economic. Worth noting is that the rise of this 'interventionist state' – the Keynesian 'consensus' or 'settlement' – was based on what was taken to be the weaknesses and limitations of the market, not a rejection of capitalist markets *per se*. However, what is also important to realize is that the Keynesian welfare state, though contradictory and complex, brought real and important benefits to working people and other disadvantaged groups. While government intervention preserved an economic system with inherent privileges for the wealthy, at the same time it was obligated to minimize social inequalities.

Today, the New Right argues that government must pull back from the public sector and market regulation, rejecting its previous Keynesian responsibilities: (1) to maintain a robust public sector; (2) to provide the general conditions for economic growth; and (3) to minimize the extent and impact of social inequalities (Lauder 1991; Brown *et al.* 1997). However, we maintain that the New Right is actually calling only for reductions in the social sphere; for example, in areas of public aid (including health provision), public education, and environmental protection. At the same time, New Right adherents overlook the government's role, funded by taxpayer revenue: (1) in saving wealthy investors, banks and corporations from bankruptcy; (2) in allocating billions of dollars for military programs; and (3) for publicly subsidizing corporate research and development.

The myopia of neoliberal freedom and opportunity

The New Right is not monolithic and there are those, for example, who argue against any kind of government intervention in the economy, seeing this as artificial, regardless of the outcome. However, our point is that it is important to distinguish between the New Right's rhetoric and its programs, which appear designed to protect those who are already privileged. This becomes evident by examining how the market is both political and economic, involving domination and coercion as well as opportunity and choice. For example, while a capitalist economic system aims primarily at maximizing corporate wealth, some argue that this is also a means for providing for the poor. Its 'trickle-down' economic theory assumes that generation of 'private' wealth subsidizes the 'public' good. Proponents of this theory maintain that government support (in the form of subsidies, tax breaks and low-interest loans) should mostly go to large-scale business instead of poor communities (in the form of unemployment benefits, jobs, or low-income housing). Indeed, this 'support' is also frequently extended to elite individuals; for example, many of the world's wealthiest businesspeople pay little in the form of personal income tax, yet they continue to benefit from the state's provision of roads, hospitals, universities and so on.

The rationale that justifies these anomalies is that the well-being of the general populace is best ensured when corporations and those who run them are provided with the best possible conditions under which to freely develop and expand. Yet, such assertions are clearly dispelled by recent economic growth in several western nations, which is accompanied by a growing income gap, continued long-term unemployment and the casualization of work, particularly in the teenage labour market but also for other workers. Such gross disparities of wealth and power – outcomes of these economic and social arrangements – are taken as 'facts of life' by the New Right. They are not cause for alarm, but evidence of others' just rewards! Indeed, one's social class, gender and/or race/ethnicity are not considered to be barriers to economic or social mobility (Aronowitz 1997). Rather, inequalities are viewed as a natural and inevitable aspect of life, given that some individuals make wrong choices, simply do not have the necessary talent or ability, or do not expend the effort needed to succeed.

This is what is typically meant by narrow capitalist versions or visions of 'democracy': to engage with the market without restraint, including without being restrained by others.

This key component of the New Right owes its allegiance to neoliberalism – a reworking of classical economics (fathered by Adam Smith) and liberal political ideals that link the virtues of the free market to individual freedom. Neoliberals propose the expulsion of the state from the market because they regard markets as a less wasteful and more efficient means of distributing goods and services within society, including the provision of education. But significantly, their concerns are also about individuals' freedom to engage with that market. While state institutions are coercive, markets are believed to occupy an idyllic sphere of society, one of opportunity, freedom and choice. From this perspective, markets are an unambiguous benefit. On the other hand, state-run education institutions, such as schools and education systems are assumed to be inherently unaccountable, in large part because of the control and self-interest that state-employed professionals (teachers being the quintessential example) and other state employees exercise in their workplace. Their role, therefore, is seen as best confined to maintaining those conditions most auspicious for the effective functioning of the market. Unencumbered by the state, individuals have the freedom to focus on their own lives and those nearest to them.

In short, free-market theorists view the market as embodying positive values – such as effort, risk taking and 'virtuous self-interest' (Novak 1982) – and as a neutral mechanism or exchange process that is self-regulating and which is capable of determining the proper relationship between supply and demand, establishing 'equitable' prices, output and even influencing methods of production. As for government, its support for and regulation of social services is viewed as an artificial intervention, as interference in what would otherwise be subject to the 'free' hand of the market. That is, market proponents argue that the state today is too unwieldy and politicized and should be restructured to reduce resources for the public sector and play a weaker regulatory role in society. This would free the market to achieve greater efficiency (spend less money) and effectiveness (get 'better' results) in as many sectors of society as possible, including education. Some neoliberals also claim that markets are inherently fair, to the extent that they provide incentives and competition, while others argue that 'fairness' is not the objective. Instead, markets ensure more creativity, cheaper products and more efficient production processes.

A rising tide of wealth does not raise all boats

As noted above, there are important discrepancies between markets in their ideal and actual states. One glaring contradiction is the increasing concentration of wealth among a few individuals and fewer corporations, while bankruptcy has become a more common experience for individuals as well as companies. This undermines claims that capitalism rewards the efforts of all hard-working, enterprising individuals. Another contradiction is the proliferation of monopolies. Monopolies are antithetical to the free market because they can manipulate supply and demand and fix the price and the quality of products. Yet today, transnational corporations control entire nations, dominate markets and overturn free competition as postulated by classical economic theory. Still, many of these corporations do not wish the state to withdraw from markets altogether. They need social regulation to maintain the environment in which they operate and to appeal for subsidies when they need to be bailed out of their (often self-inflicted) financial woes. What is not always readily acknowledged, then, is that aberrations of market theory – economic concentration, monopolies and the global domination of capital – have resulted in gross disparities in terms of living standards, income and opportunities and in the extent to which the benefits of production are available to all members of civil society.

These ever-widening inequalities of wealth and power raise the question as to whether comprehensive social programs are, as market advocates claim, necessarily a deterrent to economic efficiency, effectiveness and growth. 'Free' market policies have unleashed economic forces that have devastated many long-established industries, decimating communities that depended upon them and provoking social unrest. Precisely because today's markets have proven incapable of meeting many basic needs for the vast majority – as cartels and protectionism have demonstrated – nowhere in the industrialized world is the market allowed to operate freely. Nevertheless, it is important to point out that, historically, the human impact of the market has been contradictory; positive effects become apparent mostly in the longer term. For example, as a result of market influences, women have been provided with employment opportunities in much fuller and wider ways than have usually been possible in non-market spheres.[1] Yet, while it is possible for capitalist markets to lend themselves toward renewed growth and development (consider, for example, the influence of community banks in parts of India, Bangladesh and other countries in the region) and while they may provide variety and efficiency in production, they also produce high resource wastage in the duplication of products, advertising and fraudulent transactions (for example, stock and energy traders in the United States), as well as unacceptable inequalities in the conditions of life, causing much suffering in the process.

Reflecting on these matters, many are tempted to ask, 'can't we have *both* social justice (equity) *and* economic well-being?' Stilwell (1993: 68), for example, argues that there is no support for the idea of an equity-efficiency trade-off but that this debate is political in nature, determined by political choice, institutional arrangements and the distribution of power.[2] Surely it is possible and increasingly necessary to consciously create a more effective and rational way of organizing social and economic life. The barriers to providing social justice and well-being for all are neither technical nor material; rather, they are political and ideological. This is clearly evident when we consider that the awesome powers of contemporary production techniques unleashed by the post-Fordist scientific/technical revolution, could easily meet the material needs of all people on the globe. Yet, as long as an elite minority monopolizes extravagant wealth, poverty will be the lot of the immense majority. We wish to say this clearly because many people assume that the economy is something that ordinary people have no real control over or that the present economic system is the best possible and/or is eternal.

Re-forming education in the marketplace

In fact, rethinking and reworking the ways in which we arrange the economy and relate it to education have always been on the public agenda, although in some periods these have appeared more 'settled' than others. The 1980s, in particular, witnessed a concerted challenge (mobilized largely by the 'New Right') to the existing liberal consensus around the nature of education, including the best means of delivering it. At that time, arguments abounded in many western nations that the public sector should be dismantled or greatly reduced in size – in the name of greater efficiency and effectiveness – including proposals to make schools more like businesses, freeing them to function in the (idealized) free market economy. This extension of market logic into education was evident in such imperatives as: (1) stimulating competition among schools to break the public school 'monopoly'; (2) evoking notions of 'choice', which implied that academic achievement problems can be solved by establishing competition for students; and (3) increasing parental choice over what and where children learn. Importantly, public schools were vulnerable to many of these challenges given their reputation for unnecessary bureaucratic constraints (see Chapter 3), a perceived and often real lack of professional accountability (see Chapter 5), the isolation of teachers and schools from their surrounding communities (see Chapters 5 and 6), and embattled teacher unions. In other words, actual circumstances that existed in some schools and school districts provided a ready target for promoting New Right rhetoric on the efficiency of the free market model. Identifying public schools as the primary reason for economic weakness or cultural decline provided politicians with more manageable and less controversial solutions than would be possible were the focus on larger, more embracing economic issues.

Government strategies to reform schools, which employ discourses informed by business and market ideologies, are characterized by a customer-oriented ethos, decisions driven by efficiency and cost-effectiveness and a search for a competitive edge or advantage. As applied to education, these discourses emphasize individual relations by marginalizing teacher unions, by advocating technical rationality and competition and by employing and informing administrators from the field of business management (Gewirtz *et al.* 1995: 94). As explained above, while particular applications vary from country to country, generally the state is encouraged to intervene less directly in public arenas such as education while nevertheless retaining critical influence via accountability schemes and 'target-setting' (Whitty *et al.* 1998; Thrupp 1999). Markets in education, we are told, will raise standards, improve academic performance and – some advocates maintain – also promote equal opportunities.

Also central to these New Right prescriptions for education is the 'freedom to choose', which is perhaps the leading demand for educational reform today, popular amongst politicians and many families. The idea that parents should be able to choose which schools their children attend is manifested in various forms in England, Wales, New Zealand, Australia and the United States. More empirical studies of the consequences of specific choice schemes are needed, as well as clarity about to what standards the education system should be held accountable (Brighouse 2000). Nevertheless, it would be a profound mistake to ignore the studies of choice schemes conducted to date demonstrating that rather than improving standards, as the market model predicts they will, bad schools get worse as families with more material resources and dominant cultural capital leave (Brint 1998; Whitty *et al.* 1998; Lauder *et al.* 1999). Indeed, the research suggests that the remaining students are often 'ghettoized' in specific schools according to race, ethnicity and/or social class (Moore and Davenport 1990; Lauder *et al.* 1995).

Understandably, in this climate principals have become increasingly concerned with public relations and financial management (Bowe *et al.* 1992). Rather than inform parents and draw on their knowledge of their own children to improve education, many schools have become engaged in manipulating images in order to attract parents and students. As one principal of a low-income public high school explained: 'We have to get our own students . . . so we do, in fact, recruit and we do have to have the bells and whistles that are going to motivate students to come to us.'

It is not hard to imagine in such a context that schools would seek out academically more able students, given that they would be less costly and more likely to produce 'good' performance outcomes (Gewirtz *et al.* 1995; Glatter *et al.* 1997). Market democracy, driven by performance goals, generates pressures on schools to prioritize those students who are most likely to succeed academically. The suggestion, then, is that neoliberal economics privileges the interests of the market over equity and democratic participation. As Marginson (1997) maintains, this is because markets in education are an extension of capitalist production, consumption and exchange into areas of life once supported by government institutions. More specifically, markets:

> . . . are constituted by systems of domination-subordination and control, and help to constitute such systems in return . . . Consumer sovereignty is limited to choice between pre-given alternatives, and needs are partly defined by producers . . . In market exchange the purpose is unequal exchange . . . Market power is distributed unequally, determined by prior

inequalities in capital holdings and other attributes making for competitive success. Market competition favours the already advantaged.

(Marginson 1997: 15–16)

In short, markets presume certain competencies (dominant cultural capital)
and material possibilities, despite the fact that these are unevenly distributed
across the population. Complicating parental choice is the fact that its meaning and implications vary between classes (Gewirtz *et al.* 1995); markets
strategically reassert the privileges of the middle and ruling classes, including racial and ethnic advantages, which have been threatened by previous
education reforms (Ball 1993).

'New Managerialism': consumer governance

In the context of the rise of neoliberalism, the valorization of the market
model and reduced public expenditures on health, education and welfare –
most notably during the past two decades – public education systems in
many western countries have witnessed a new emphasis on management.
This 'new managerialism' (Clarke *et al.* 1994) has granted more control
functions to individual schools even though the state has retained its pre-
rogative and capacity for control via more rigorous accountability and funding schemes. Also referred to as 'corporate managerialism' (Considine 1988;
Yeatman 1998b, 1990), it has provided a focus on outcomes rather than
inputs or processes and includes in its vocabulary reference to customers,
empowerment, charters, innovation and excellence. As an ideology, new or
corporate managerialism implies a critique of both professional and bureaucratic control over schools; the two are often configured as one interlocking
set of power relations. From this perspective, these particular power relations
are criticized for enshrining monopoly-like features in public schools with
self-interested professionals unaccountable to others; particularly to business but also, more vocally, to parents and students. The new managerialism
thus proposes changing both how schools are governed as well as their
internal culture (Deem *et al.* 1995: 32–3). An 'enterprise culture' (Heelas
and Morris 1992) is intended to replace a public sector ethos with an atmos-
phere more akin to private business, encouraging individuals not to be held
back by bureaucratic regulations but instead to use their personal initiative
to transform teaching and learning. Considine explains this broad cultural
shift in the public sector as:

a major project of modernisation and rationalisation which reworks
and intensifies aspects of the operational techniques of the established
paradigm of technical rationality, shifting its emphasis from the legal to
the economic and from values of protection and compensation to those
of competition and entrepreneurialism.

(Considine 1988: 6)

More recent analyses[3] raise serious concerns about some of these underlying premises of managerialism. One concern is that there seems no clear
connection between marketized forms of managing schools and students'
outcomes. Even Caldwell, one of the strongest proponents of 'market devolution' (Lingard *et al.* 2002) in Australian education, has admitted:

> There is no doubt that, while factors underpinning the movement to
> self-managing schools are many and varied, there has always been an
> expectation that they will make a contribution to improved outcomes
> for students. There is also no doubt that evidence of a direct cause-and-
> effect relationship between self-management and improved outcomes
> is minimal. This is understandable given that few initiatives in self-
> management have been linked in a systematic way to what occurs in
> classrooms in a manner that is likely to impact on learning.
>
> (Caldwell 1998: 38)

In short, other than the observation above that schools can improve student
outcomes by soliciting students more likely to achieve academic success –
'poaching' them from other school districts – market forms of school management are yet to be linked to improved outcomes for students.

A second concern is the conception of the public as disaggregated, independent individuals who are free to endlessly choose and consume commodities, including education (Peters *et al.* 2000: 120). In this account, there
is no such thing as society, only individuals and their jobs – if they have
them. Such notions effectively deny or ignore the importance of social classes
and other distinct social groups in understanding social and economic
relations. Viewing society as nothing but individuals gathered in the marketplace obscures questions of material inequality, namely unpaid work (done
mostly by women), low-paid work and the inequalities between those
owning the majority of productive property and the working population
(Levitas 1996). Differences in the resources people *bring to* the market are
effectively ignored or denied.

Another way of denying or ignoring the importance of group identity and
heritage is evident in what the market *utilizes*. For example, the State of
California recently voted down a measure that would prohibit high schools
from using such names as 'Redskins' or 'Braves' for their sport teams. The
argument was that individual schools should have the right to name their
teams anything they wanted, regardless of the claims made by indigenous
Americans about the offensiveness of such terms. The groups that successfully defeated the measure to restrict these 'naming rights' did not have to
justify to 'others' – who represented different and marginalized standpoints
(Young 1990: 190) – the compatibility of their 'right' with more general
principles of social justice. While many people may wish to remain blind to
'difference' and to pursue their own interests irrespective of the cost to others,
on the contrary we think that group representation is necessary to ensure
effective recognition and inclusion of those perspectives that are typically
marginalized or oppressed. When society is recognized as comprising diverse

classes and oppressed social groups, more opportunities present themselves for increasing the knowledge available for public deliberations.[4] These are matters to which we return in Chapter 6.

A central assumption of new managerialism, then, is that *individual* freedom to choose and consume is the highest form of freedom to be desired. Moreover, possibilities for people to meaningfully engage with society through institutions other than the labour market are discounted (Levitas 1996). Indeed, vocational accounts of the purposes of education currently dominate the thinking of many students, their parents and teachers (see Gale and Densmore 2000). However, we think a more comprehensive freedom would exist were we to ensure the necessary material, social and economic conditions so that all people's needs are met and they are provided with opportunities to reach their potential. This notion of rights acknowledges that a particular kind of social or public life, namely one without want, is necessary in order for individuals to be free. Whereas, under new managerialism, the conditions under which people choose and consume receive little scrutiny, including any constraints affecting these. Some scholars, therefore, associate market managerialism with a form of governance where individuals believe themselves to be autonomous choosers while underestimating the extent to which the structure of the market and the extension of market theories to principles of education – as well as to other areas of life – severely restrict their choices.

A third, closely related concern is that notions of social needs, social purposes and equity have played little if any part in the development of this managerialism. To the extent that equity has been a concern, it has been defined in individualistic, self-interested, consumerist terms or as related to the efficiency and/or effectiveness of production. In viewing parents as autonomous consumers, a managerialist model fails to address what kinds of communities we wish to live in and what kinds of social relations we wish to find inside schools. For instance, do most people really want maximizing individual choice in preference to democratic processes as the dominant conditions encouraging some behaviours and limiting others? We think not. Nevertheless, with increasing aspects of teaching and learning translated into performance indicators and measurable outcomes, it becomes easy to assume that that which is or can be measured is important while what cannot be measured appears to be of less value. In this way, the activities of management shape what happens between teachers and students, teachers and administrators, parents and teachers, and parents and their children. Social, economic and political problems are converted into technical ones, with technical solutions.

Open to business: selling off education to the highest bidder

This ideology informing managerialism can be contrasted to the previous socio-economic settlement, which, as late as the 1960s, held that free, compulsory and secular schools were the right of all citizens and primarily the responsibility of governments to finance and maintain. It was assumed that governments had civic duties to perform; namely, the provision of social services and, very generally, the maintenance of conditions that would contribute to the well-being of society. While schools were responsible for enabling students to be economically successful, they were viewed as equally responsible to perform certain social functions, such as preparing youth for democratic citizenship and social literacy. This notion that schooling performs a critical *social* function has its origins in the initial proposals for mass schooling in western capitalist societies. In the nineteenth century, the state provision of education came to be embraced by many working people and progressive educators throughout the United Kingdom, the United States, Australia and New Zealand as the best means to provide individual advancement for all (Williams 1961). While strengthening class control was a key motive for the establishment of public schools, at the same time working people struggled for the opening and maintenance of public schools believing that they could offer educational opportunity, help mitigate social divisions such as those of class, race, ethnicity and gender and help prepare the way for a democratic society and national prosperity (Grace 1995). Many people had faith that schools were, either actually or potentially, educating for democracy; enabling the young to function competently and intelligently in a democratic society as well as improve their employment possibilities.

Notwithstanding the wealth of critical scholarship demonstrating that education systems are intimately involved in the (re)production and preservation of social hierarchies (Dewey 1958; Connell 1993; Brint 1998), there is good reason to keep these hopes alive today. The public school ideal maintains that children's education should not be disadvantaged by their backgrounds and circumstances and that the state should provide free, quality education for all students, not simply a safety net for those unable to afford to pay for their own (private) schooling. While this has obvious importance for poor, historically oppressed peoples, the legitimacy of public schooling as an institution depends upon its effectiveness in reaching out to all students to enable them to reach their potential. Yet, early empirical studies support the argument that the market in education functions as a class strategy, securing educational advantage for those who are already privileged, at the expense of the poor (Marginson 1993, 1997; Whitty *et al.* 1998; Thrupp 1999), and that race and ethnic inequalities are also exacerbated (Darden *et al.* 1992; Lauder *et al.* 1999).

It is primarily for this reason that the relative importance assigned by the New Right to markets for providing education (and social services) has to be questioned. At the very least, markets have been grossly exaggerated as the single primary criteria for delivering effectiveness and efficiency in education. Moreover, while much of the current economic rhetoric gives lip service to individual rights and their importance in a democracy, New Right economics actually embodies anti-democratic orientations and proposals. For instance, market theorists claim that education is best viewed as a commodity to be sold, a peculiar mixing of the public and private sectors (see Chapter 6). In this account, students and their parents are viewed as consumers with the option to make choices for themselves about which school to attend. The primary purpose of education from this perspective is to maximize individual opportunity for economic advancement. This is the logic of a competitive economic system, which necessarily ensures that consumers will only get the education they can afford, irrespective of ability and need.

A second example of the anti-democratic premise of New Right economics is the promotion of the interests of corporate wealth above the public's welfare. As noted above, corporate wealth does not tend to 'trickle down' to the poor nor do commodities, produced for the purpose of profitable sales, prioritize social well-being. Nevertheless, competitive social relations driven by profit motives now permeate and commodify nearly every aspect of our lives. For example, in the USA, some businesses supplement the funding of poor schools, provided the school daily subjects its students to product advertisements. These relations determine not only what will be produced and consumed within schools and their communities but also our leisure and resources. While the social and political have always been related to the economic in one form or another (Althusser 1969), emotional, aesthetic and spiritual qualities of life (museums, concerts, marriage and so on) are increasingly constrained by and conceived within fiscal considerations. Today's dominant worldview suggests that every social sphere is a marketplace, that all organizations and institutions should be run like businesses and that important human interactions are themselves essentially economic transactions.

Student achievement, school accountability and collective 'rights'

Viewing education as 'a choice for consumers' contrasts sharply with viewing it as 'a right of citizens' (Grace 1994: 132). Choice – freedom of and more of – has, under neoliberalism, become a cardinal value, yet ascribing rights to consumers according to their wealth conflicts with the full entitlements of citizenry. Actively choosing material goods, social services, values, lifestyles, indeed identities, has signalled new freedoms for the endowed; there can be positive elements to a perceived autonomous self. The New Right, however, has successfully used free market policies and the discourses of the marketplace to limit democracy for many to notions of consumer choice. This prioritizes the individualistic, competitive and consumerist components of what might otherwise constitute a (different) kind of 'active citizenship'. Given such a different conception, individual choices about which school to send one's children, for example, might be made only after larger community interests and other families' interests have been taken into account. It might also mean that for the foreseeable future the state will have to play an active role, if equity is to develop and expand throughout all school systems (Lauder 1990; Hatcher 1996; Whitty *et al.* 1998).

Our point, then, is not what is the best way to combat institutional stagnation, unleash initiative or improve a school's academic performance, nor how these goals are best approached, even though these are legitimate matters of concern. Rather, we think that it is important to first distinguish between two fundamentally different notions of individual freedoms or rights: (1) where the rights of an individual to choose are assumed to be pitted against the perceived equal rights of others – the right to compete and secure advantages for oneself over others, and (2) where the rights of an individual are viewed as necessarily involving others, namely those with whom we are in relation. The second notion maintains that democratic individual freedoms or rights can only be established in the context of social relations (Laclau and Mouffe 2001: 185). From this perspective, radical democratic rights presuppose the existence of equal rights for others and can only truly be exercised collectively. The existence of equal rights presumes certain material resources, particularly food, shelter, income, health care and education for all. The underlying assumption is that without these resources people are unable to participate fully in the life of society. Nowhere in the industrialized world has the market been able to provide these basic needs for all of society, much less in an equitable manner.

Adopting the second conception of rights would necessitate extensive public discussion and debate about whether we truly desire schools in which all students can academically and personally 'achieve' and, if so, whether we are willing to ensure the necessary conditions in order for this to occur. Because we live in an unjust society, resistance of the privileged to this idea is predictable, even understandable. As Thrupp (1999) argues, opposition from the middle and ruling classes to measures designed to bring about greater equality should not be underestimated. The problem is that improving the funding of poor schools is likely to mean taking some of the resources out of middle- and ruling-class schools in order to direct them to poor schools (Whitty *et al.* 1998). Or, as recently attempted in New Jersey, there could be equitable funding across all school districts, regardless of the property tax base. However, the formula utilized by the current Australian conservative government to fund schools also makes claims about the equitable allocation of resources, as a way of justifying the distribution of millions of dollars to the nation's elite private schools.

However, rather than grappling with complex issues of providing all schools with the enormously expanded and consistent funding base they need (see Anyon 1997), politicians and policy makers have proffered more simplistic formulas for reform, especially those tied to standardized testing.[5] For example, many schools in the United States are now faced with being closed down or 'restructured' if their students fail to achieve certain test scores. Federally mandated annual testing is the cornerstone of newly approved bipartisan policies for public schools. Sanctions for schools that fail to meet federally determined targets include various 'corrective measures' including state takeover or transferring the management of schools to private contractors (Karp 2002: 3). With their introduction, President Bush has retreated from his stated commitment to 'reduce' government and unleash market forces and has instead instituted a bigger role for the federal government. Significantly, this expanded federal role is likely to cause greater school failure, given that the standards schools are required to meet are often unrealistic, inappropriate and underfunded. Greater school failure will in turn feed into the neoliberal critique of public education as a failed state monopoly best remedied by its privatization. This is more than ironic; it reveals groundwork that is being laid for privatization. It also reveals a change in the federal government's role from a promoter of access and equity in public education to the promotion of an agenda that is likely to exacerbate existing social inequalities.

We agree that in many areas a concern with poor academic performance is long overdue but we do not believe a student's total knowledge and ability can be defined simply through test scores. Doing well on standardized tests does not necessarily mean you will succeed in university/college, enjoy your job, be an active member of your community, or be an imaginative, critical thinker engaged in complex problem solving and social critique. Along with many teachers, we worry that a concern with academic performance, as measured by standardized testing, emphasizes the development of test-taking skills and defines learning principally in terms of procedure over substance. For both teachers and students, this downplays the content of what is to be understood and what is to be done. The social and political functions of education remain concealed, further limiting sophisticated, comprehensive discussion on educational issues. Test scores will not help us address the inequities of the resegregation in urban schools or the reduced access to higher education for the poor and students of colour. While holding teachers, administrators and students to high expectations is a healthy challenge, and while the neoliberal approach can bring money into some schools, still, the underlying causes of why students perform poorly must be addressed in order to effect lasting change. However, given the private enterprise model for education, the prospects appear grim for broadening the current discourse around testing, school vouchers and accountability schemes to include issues related to the economic rehabilitation and stabilization of neighbourhoods and values that speak to a democratic society. As long as this is the case, we can expect a tiered educational system.

To reiterate, school-based reforms are legitimate concerns, especially for low-income students. Reforms that help parents and community members know how well their children are learning and how well their schools are performing are especially important. But to suggest that standardized tests, for example, can answer these questions, is yet to be borne out by research. Teachers, parents, students and interested others need to be involved in discussions about alternative means of assessment as well as other potential reforms (see Chapter 3). And, in contrast to an approach that says that school-based remedies themselves are capable of effectiveness regardless of their context, we need an approach that incorporates the many factors influencing student outcomes. Addressing youth employment, minimum wages, swing-shift jobs and deteriorating neighbourhoods has the potential to reverse those structural inequalities in society that undermine even the best attempts at school reform. Whereas school reforms that only address what occurs inside schools are not likely to produce an educational system capable of preparing all youth for functioning in a robust democratic society nor in a competitive economy.

Conclusion

As indicated in Chapter 1, we see our inquiry in this chapter and the ones that follow as part of a critical tradition that engages with educational issues in relation to larger societal problems, an engagement with both local and global issues. Our theoretical supposition is that when educational change and socio-economic change are treated as dialectically related processes, we can best understand not only what is actually going on inside schools but also explore possibilities for desirable reforms. In this vein we have argued that individual freedom and laissez-faire economics are reversing much of the progress that had been made towards establishing a more democratic and just society, while at the same time recognizing that such 'progress' itself has been disjointed and fractured and not without need for improvement. Just one indication of this flight from social justice is the rising segregation in our schools based on socio-economic status (SES), even though we now know that the greater the social mix among a school's student body, the better most students will perform (McPherson and Willms 1987; Lauder and Hughes 1990; Thrupp 1997, 1999). In part, this segregation is a product of the pressures on schools to provide individuals with social advantage, which have taken precedence over goals associated with maintaining and enhancing public life (Labaree 1997). Related to this, we have also noted that market logic is informed by competitive self-interest. In our view, however, individuals' 'self'-interest often merges with general or common interests, even where this is not recognized. In this sense, contributing to the 'common good' or social betterment strengthens individual rights. Perhaps a distinction between self-interest and selfish interest might help us identify criteria for making normative judgements about the relative value of competing practices, judgements and social relations. Without such a distinction some people pose self-interest as a moral defect or, more commonly, believe that competitive social relations with a focus on securing personal advantage over others is 'natural'. We think it is important to examine how this belief has become part of the public discourse and, perhaps more importantly, whether striving for relative advantage is the highest aim to which we might aspire.

As implied at the beginning of this chapter, questions about the appropriateness of applying market principles to education are primarily centred around issues of social and economic justice. The question for education, therefore, is not only what is the most appropriate mechanism for providing education but also what are the goals of public education. We believe that all children should be provided with a sound and basic education so that they can grow and flourish as persons in the making. In our view, 'standards' need not be equated with high-stakes standardized tests. Rather, they should focus on improving high-quality academic learning for all students. A sound and basic education for all students would also necessitate a variety of enriching programmes, higher paid teachers, better physical facilities and smaller classes in most public schools. New formulas for school funding are urgently needed.

We also think that schools should function as micro-communities where the abilities to work with and learn from diverse others and to collectively discuss social problems and alternative solutions can develop (see Chapter 6). Towards that end, high-quality learning would be facilitated by increasing the number of teachers of colour and teachers who are able to promote an anti-racist and social justice perspective. With regard to the latter, teachers would teach their students to analyse the various discourses operating in society and the benefits and limitations they pose. Also, we recognize that voucher systems and some charter schools appear to many parents as the best way to provide their children with the education they deserve. Unfortunately, the main impact of both of these 'innovations' will be to siphon money away from many public schools, leaving them with even fewer resources. The relatively privileged will move to private schools, increasing segregation within and between schools. The limits of the marketplace to provide schools that function for the benefit of all citizens make it incumbent upon us to explore non-market possibilities for reaching these goals, for combating school and community segregation and for challenging the widespread over-valuing of consumer activity.

At the heart of our discussion, then, we are critical of the current dominant view of an education system premised on market principles. For many people, the economy is not an area of life to which we can readily apply the criteria of democracy, even if we wanted. Either the economy appears to have its own 'natural' laws and rights or to be something that individuals should approach as individuals, not as groups of people with common interests. Market economies, however, like all economies, embody social relations. Certain interests are protected at the expense of others. Markets are created, restructured, regulated, reduced and/or destroyed. Hence, a market-like system of schooling is not preordained, but is a political decision. Current pressures to replace public education by a marketplace system, limiting the role of the public to making an individual 'choice' to attend a particular school, are based on an idealization of commodity markets, exploiting the myth that profit incentives in education will answer the failures of public schools.

Those concerned with social justice issues must examine the nature of the social relations set into motion by a market economy. For example, how is consumer-like behaviour altering public institutions, civic duty, community service, life in neighbourhoods and even the quality of intimate relationships? The problem is that market economics and the glorification of privatization and choice undermine the possibilities for democracy and vital public life. In contrast, a radical democratic culture and compassionate socio-economic order value individuals who are not motivated by greed or selfishness but who place the protection of all human lives and the natural and social environment above the right of individuals to limitless personal wealth. Markets might be used to exchange some goods and services but not those necessities upon which people depend in order to live a life with dignity. Certain social goods and services could be allocated according to need in order to raise the material base of life for everyone and to ensure greater social justice. This would not have to necessitate an oppressive state government. A network of local institutions, well integrated into various levels of government, could give access to all people to debate and determine local priorities and policies for providing services and otherwise determine what is needed and useful, including in the field of education.[6]

This level and quality of democracy would allow communities to create mechanisms for engaging in discussion and decision making on what economic arrangements might look like were our economy to produce for the benefit of the majority of families, rather than for profit making by a wealthy minority. As Dorothy Shipps (2000) suggests, urban public school failure might be best understood as a product of the demise of the public sphere rather than as the result of administrative failure and the lack of choice. Shipps (2000: 104) argues that such an understanding could emphasize the benefits of full public participation in a democracy, embracing equity as a common concern and education (as with the rest of urban infrastructure) as a source of community pride. After all, as Labaree (2000) reminds us, even those families who send their children to private schools benefit from quality public education systems. All of us stand to benefit when public schools graduate competent, knowledgeable young adults, respectful of and able to work with others.

Dominant ideologies, informed by the hyperbole of the market and consumerism, make claims about how the world *should* work, about what the nature of education *should* be, and about *desirable* outcomes of an education system. Under the guise of defending individual liberty, neoliberalism legitimizes an individualistic definition of freedom and rights that might have been suited to previous historical eras. Today, however, the dominant ideology helps marginalize basic questions about and means for publicly defining the democratic values and social justice aims with which we wish to shape our school system and the larger society. In this chapter we hope we have challenged the assumption that schooling should almost exclusively serve individual needs and/or those of the economy, particularly as these are defined by business. Similarly, we hope we have encouraged educators and educational institutions to emphasize more than that which is simply ascribed importance by standardized tests and more than that which is seen to be of benefit to individuals alone. In our view, re-emphasizing cooperative social relations and the collective interests of social groups is the place to begin the democratization of education.

Questions for discussion/research

- What do the specific conditions within a particular school suggest about the possibilities for resistance to market pressures?
- What do we need to understand about capital, finance and markets to better understand how schooling reproduces inequalities?
- Is there some meaning of 'choice' which could further social justice?
- What are the limits to education serving as an instrument for equal entry into top jobs?
- How do markets interact with the positional character of education?
- In what ways might a democratic economy facilitate the realization of democratic schooling?

Suggested readings

Lingard, B., Hayes, D. and Mills, M. (2002) Developments in school-based management. The specific case of Queensland, Australia, *Journal of Educational Administration*, 40(1): 6–30.

Marginson, S. (1997) *Markets in Education*. St. Leonards, NSW: Allen & Unwin, Chapter 2.

Slee, R., Weiner, G. with Tomlinson, S. (eds) (1998) *School Effectiveness for Whom?* London: Falmer Press, Chapters 2 and 3.

Stoll, L. and Myers, K. (eds) (1998) *No Quick Fixes: Perspectives on Schools in Difficulty*. London: Falmer Press, Chapter 5.

_____ *three* _____

Policy: the authoritative allocation of values

Teachers sometimes regard education policy as a *fait accompli*, which leaves them with few alternatives but to embrace it – a palatable option if the policy resonates with a teacher's own values – or reject it and be left 'out in the cold' with no authority to question its legitimacy. For teachers who value a socially just and democratic education for their students, policies that propose otherwise pose such a dilemma. This chapter suggests that their predicament is sometimes born of conceptions of policy that separate it from practice and which are devoid of tactical forms of engagement. For other teachers, misconceptions of policy are based in experiences of being treated as policy objects; 'false' consciousness, it must be remembered, is based in real, day-to-day activities and experiences. Addressing these two concerns, we make the case for teachers as policy producers and examine the tactics they might employ in negotiating policy. These are explored within the context of student assessment policy, particularly the 'imposition' of standardized testing: policy that is illustrative of the conjoining of conservative and neoliberal arms of New Right politics in its regulation of teachers, its contributions to the marketization of educational institutions and its regard for students as human capital. That is, while the policy rhetoric is concerned with students' academic achievement, many believe it is also interested in making teachers and students accountable to the interests of business and in deflecting public criticism away from government.

Guiding questions/issues

At a broader level, this is the contradiction explored in this chapter: how to address policy that claims to address the interests of many yet is produced by and seems more focused on serving the interests of a few. In the context of teachers and schooling, we approach these issues by asking:

- What is policy?
- What is policy making?
- How are teachers positioned in making policy for schooling?
- How can teachers engage in the policy-making process?

The first two of these are addressed throughout the chapter. They are intimately related: policy is influenced in character by how it is made. They are also explored in relation to teachers as policy makers. The first section of the chapter is concerned with how teachers are out-positioned in the policy-making process, whereas the second focuses on how teachers might engage with policy in contexts of practice; in de Certeau's (1984) terms, how teachers employ 'tactics' to undermine policy and/or imagine different 'uses' for policy.[1] Data utilized in the chapter are drawn from a case study of an Australian high school. The research focused on teachers', parents' and students' engagement with schooling, the strategies they employed in reworking this to suit their own values and circumstances, and the space available for them to do so. The full data set includes semi-structured interviews with most of the schools' teachers and approximately 10 per cent of its parents and students, although in this chapter only the principal's voice is heard and only in relation to policies of national standardized testing. In our view, concentrating on one key participant allows for a coherent storyline to emerge of how at least one teacher understands the role of teachers as policy makers. At the time of the study, Pam (not her real name) was the principal of the school, situated in a disadvantaged community. Previous to this appointment, she had had a long career in teaching, including working in primary/elementary schools, with students with learning difficulties and as a project officer working across school sectors and communities.

Out-positioning teachers in the policy-making process

Defining policy as the 'authoritative allocation of values' (Easton 1953; Anderson 1979) is useful in drawing attention to the *who* and the *how* of policy production. Prunty has argued similarly, that 'The authoritative allocation of values draws our attention to the centrality of power and control in the concept of policy, and requires us to consider not only *whose* values are represented in policy, but also *how* these values have become institutionalised' (1985: 136, emphasis added).

Such considerations are important because they expose the partiality (and, hence, fallacy) of rationality and consensus in policy production, or at least make room for such disclosure. In our view, traditional representations of the democratic process, in which policy is produced through mutual agreement (consensus reached through rational debate) while authority to produce it is invested in elected representatives (often supported by technical expertise) – consigning all else and others to the domains of implementation and consumption – are both theoretically naïve and demonstrably undemocratic. As a way of redressing this elitist politics, drawing attention to the *who* of policy production enables the naming of values inherent in things that are seemingly technical (such as policy) and the foregrounding of a radical democracy (Lummis 1996) – which engages all people in public processes – as a legitimate basis for policy's authority. Whereas, drawing attention to the *how* of policy production challenges not just the premise of rationality in policy making but also how particular individuals and groups are involved in various contexts as policy *producers*. In brief, the who and how of policy production are dialectically related.

In this section we particularly focus on who are currently legitimated as policy makers in producing policy for schooling. In part, this is to remind ourselves and others that policy has a face. Policy may present itself as universal, generalized and even commonsensical but its interests and influence are invariably partial. In particular, we consider how teachers are out-positioned by their de-legitimation as policy makers, their voices dismissed as self-interested (see also Chapters 2 and 5).

Traditional and contemporary faces of policy: few of them look like teachers

Traditionally, permission to speak policy has been vested in the state. In the academic literature, for example, definitions of policy often carry references to the state or to government[2] as a way of framing what is legitimate policy and what is not, or what is not of particular significance. This literature also refers to distinctions such as *public* policy and *education* policy as ways of demarcating policy from other socio-political activities and actors. Many of these definitions are informed by 'executive' models of policy production, whereas others adopt a 'partnership' model (Yeatman 1998a) and, hence, different conceptions of the nature of the state and how this defines the positioning of policy actors. Some extend this examination to questioning the legitimacy and adequacy of the state itself in producing policy in post-modern societies (see Dale 1992; Hoffman 1995). Others note that the rhetoric of withering nation states and policy relevance under the influence of market globalization is not simply matched by empirical evidence (Keating and Davis 2000).

Such distinctions are informed by matters of *policy speak*: what is considered legitimate to say in policy contexts. Even though 'policy' and 'politics' are derived from the same root word (from the ancient Greek city-state, or *polis*) and are indistinguishable in several European languages (*politik* in German; *politique* in French, and so on), some still view policy as 'concerned with outcomes, whereas politics is concerned with process and, in particular, with the participants' position in the game' (Colebatch 1998: 73). We return below to such talk of positions and games but in a way that gives recognition to the politics of the policy process. Rather than viewing policy as static, the understanding here is that it invites its own distinctive type of politics that is 'internal to the policy process and is shaped by it' (Yeatman 1998a: 22). In particular, it is a politics that speaks of a desired future: 'policy occurs when social actors think about what they are doing and why *in relation to different and alternative possible futures*' (Yeatman 1998a: 19, emphasis added). Clearly, these are matters that also occupy the thoughts and practices of teachers, even though this is not always legitimated by their inclusion in producing official policy documents. This is despite the fact that policy – what Michel Foucault would refer to as forms of power – is what gets realized and reproduced through social interaction, within the everyday life of institutions (Ball 1994a).

Such discussions are about the political and theoretical boundaries we draw around policy, including those who participate in its production (and those who do not) and under what conditions. The theoretical boundaries between those who produce and those who implement policy have under gone considerable debate in the policy literature (see, for example, Wilensky 1986) and are now well and truly dismissed as theoretically ill informed. Roger Dale, for example, has noted that:

> Severing implementation from formulation of policy involves not only a distortion but a serious misunderstanding of the role of the state in education policy. It is a misunderstanding connected to the view that the State involvement in education implies ownership, control and operation of education systems, with a functional division of labour between formulation and implementation of policy.
>
> (1992: 393)

But the distinction lives on in the minds of many, in hegemonic and disciplined ways that serve to privilege some policy actors and their activities in particular contexts at the expense of others. In short, advocating such separations on theoretical grounds amounts to political strategy. Yeatman, for example, notes that to define policy:

> . . . as *technical* in character . . . [is to privilege] the advice of experts not the participation of citizens. This is the function of the recent take-over of the policy agenda by libertarian neo-classical economics where the most important policy issues are represented as economic ones. This particular brand of economics is especially salient because it not only privileges the private power of business corporations who command enormous political influence but it seems to speak on behalf of the freedom of choice of the ordinary person.
>
> (Yeatman 1998a: 25, original emphasis)

What is clearly evident here is the political nature of the policy process or, more accurately, the political nature of attempts to deny the legitimacy of the policy process: the right of those who are affected by policy to be involved in its determination. Yet, in a political sense, 'for the conception of policy as a policy process to be possible, the work of state administration has to be conceived democratically' (Yeatman 1998a: 17). Here Yeatman intentionally blends politics and theory; a strategy she extends to conceptions of policy activism:

> I am offering a normative definition of *policy activist* . . . as anyone who champions in relatively consistent ways a value orientation and pragmatic

commitment to what I have called the policy process, namely a conception of policy which opens it up to the appropriate participation of all those who are involved in policy all the way through points of conception, operational formulation, implementation, delivery on the ground, consumption and evaluation.

(Yeatman 1998a: 34, original emphasis)

While we appreciate the politics here, we also understand policy activism to include the activities of those with commitments to less participatory interests; in particular, those who are committed to restricting the participation of others. As noted in Chapter 2, the efforts of the dominant to retain their dominance should not be underestimated (Thrupp 1999). However, we also acknowledge the theoretical intent of aspects of Yeatman's account, particularly her broadening of Heclo's (1978) original conception of policy activism (restricted to policy advisers) to include activists at all stages of the policy process, including teachers in schools. We could imagine, then, a pairing, as illustrated in Table 3.1, where particular policy actors dominate particular policy contexts. What is envisaged are 'key mediators of policy in any setting who are relied upon by others to relate policy to context or to gatekeep' (Ball 1994a: 17). The understanding is that 'only certain voices are heard at any point in time' (Ball 1994a: 16). This gatekeeping is well illustrated in the comments of Pam, the school principal in our research:

> . . . a policy comes out. It goes through the Senior Policy Officer who sends it out for review at district level through the people in District Office. It comes to the principal who then puts it into practice in their school . . . In a high school, that starts with the principal and deputy, and then it's a HOD's [Head of Department's] job . . . before it gets to a classroom teacher . . . [but] most teachers say 'I don't want to know about the politics, just tell me what to do'. And they don't understand then that they're getting someone else's way of interpreting that policy into their classroom.

(Pam)

Despite the suggestion in these comments and in Yeatman's (1998a: 11) listing of stages, what is not meant in Table 3.1 is a strict separation between contexts and their productive activities (see Gale 1999b) nor a linear representation of the policy process. A more cogent reading would be that as particular policy actors tend to dominate particular contexts so they are also dominated by particular activities, although not exclusively so. Policy actors and their activities cannot be pinned down indefinitely; instead, they are temporarily settled in particular contexts. Similarly, policy positions and stances are not defined simply by their material properties but can be conceived as 'different descriptions of the same social reality' (Gale 1999b: 404).

Another way of explaining these relations between policy contexts, actors and their activities is in terms of Bourdieu's notions of capital and field (see, for example, Bourdieu and Wacquant 1992: 98–9). In such terms, determining

Table 3.1 Policy-making contexts and their policy makers

Produced where? What kind of productive activity?	Produced by whom? What kind of productive vocality?
Contexts of policy making (Bowe *et al.* 1992; Ball 1994a) **Stages of the policy process** (Yeatman 1998a)	**Interest groups** (Lawton 1986) **Policy activists** (Yeatman 1998a)
• context of influence (Bowe *et al.* 1992); • setting the policy agenda and policy development (Yeatman 1998a)	• politicians (Lawton 1986); • government executives (for example, Cabinet), legislators, the judiciary (Yeatman 1998a)
• context of policy text production (Bowe *et al.* 1992); • policy formulation	• bureaucrats (Lawton 1986); • public officials – bureaucrats, public servants, public managers (Yeatman 1998a)
• context of practice (Bowe *et al.* 1992); • policy implementation and policy delivery (Yeatman 1998a)	• professionals (Lawton 1986); • Direct service deliverers – for example, those who staff a school, from principal to teachers to ancillary staff (Yeatman 1998a)
• context of outcomes (Ball 1994a)	• the consumers, users, recipients of policy and those subject to its regulation (Yeatman 1998a)
• context of political strategy (Ball 1994a); • policy evaluation and policy monitoring (Yeatman 1998a)	• policy analysts – analysis *of* and *for* policy (Gordon *et al.* 1977; Kenway 1990)

the limits of a policy field is one and the same thing as determining the capital valued within that field. In other words, at any one point in time, certain cultural, social, economic and symbolic resources (capitals) tend to dominate any one policy context. Hence, as illustrated in Table 3.1, the capital seen to be required to formulate policy documents is privileged in contexts of policy text production. Further, it is not just the volume but also the structure of one's capital that determines a policy actor's positioning (their relative force in producing policy) and their strategic and/or tactical orientation within particular policy contexts. Hence, bureaucrats and public officials, for example, might be better positioned to write policy text and, therefore, dominate contexts of policy text production because they possess more of the relevant capitals that that context values. Similarly, different forms of capital – and, therefore, what is deemed relevant – tend to dominate schools. For example, from Pam's perspective:

... the standardized tests that we're doing in school ... they really are useless. It's only what you do in observing kids' learning and what's happening in a classroom that's valid. Even when you look at kids who are going well in a classroom and you think, 'Oh, they're really going well', they can still sit an exam and fail ... The method of assessment doesn't always fit the way it's been taught ... We as educators look at it that way.

(Pam)

Bourdieu and Wacquant's (1992) analogy of a game to explain the inter-actions of and more fluid relations between (policy) actors within (policy) fields is instructive in explaining the relative authority of policy makers. In negotiating the policy process or 'game', policy actors or:

> ... players can play to increase or to conserve their capital [and, hence, their positioning in a particular policy context] ... in conformity with the tacit rules of the game and the prerequisites of the reproduction of the game and its stakes; but they can also get in it to transform, partially or completely, the immanent rules of the game. They can, for instance, work to change ... the exchange rate between various species of capital, through strategies aimed at discrediting the form of capital upon which the force of their opponents rests ... and to valorize the species of capital they preferentially possess.
>
> (Bourdieu and Wacquant 1992: 99)

Below we examine ways in which teachers can and do engage with policy to transform or remake it. Specifically, de Certeau's (1984) account of 'con-sumers' of discipline and the 'uses' and 'tactics' they employ to engage with their subordination by 'producers', is particularly helpful in explaining *how* some teachers play policy games in ways that transform not only policy but also their own positions, from policy consumers to policy producers. First, though, we outline the current value of teachers' stakes in the game, according to its current set of rules, in order to be clear about what teachers are up against when they take on policy producers.

Raising the policy-making stakes: short-changing teachers

Teachers' capital – specifically their pedagogical knowledge, which is valued primarily in schools and other education institutions – has a low exchange rate in contexts of policy text production. Indeed, teachers can sometimes feel as though they are at the sharp end of policy, that they are treated as the 'objects of policy interventions rather than as the authors of social change' (Connell 1994: 133). This view by teachers is understandable given their virtual exclusion from education policy-making forums during the 1980s and 1990s, with 'their control over meaning lost, [and] their pro-fessional preferences replaced' (Ball 1990: 18). As argued in Chapter 2, 'replacing' their interests are the interests of business, industry and market competition, but it is worth noting that the levers of social and economic control engaged by governments have also been adjusted (see Chapter 4). For example, politicians with education portfolio responsibilities are now far more inclined to inject themselves into affairs previously considered the domain of bureaucrats; a phenomenon often referred to as 'ministerialization' or the politicization of the bureaucracy. Whereas at the 'chalkface', such interventions are more often experienced as 'steering at a distance' (Kickert 1991; Marceau 1993), although the intent of policy produced by govern ment and bureaucracies is often to provide greater reach into the working lives and practices of professional educators (Gale 2000). This is to ensure that teachers 'do as they are told', that they conform to the public interest (conceived as that of the market), which is embodied in the policies of elected governments. Invoked by governments to achieve these ends are the dual policy settings of devolved responsibility (centrifugal strategies) and increased accountability (centripetal strategies), which together bind in social activity extremes and extremists.

Not surprisingly, in this context teachers often feel, and frequently are, left with few choices:

> It's very wrong but if you want to be part of the system you have to do it . . . you might be in an employment situation [with which] you very much disagree, but it's part of the agreement you have with your employer that you will implement what they decree. It doesn't mean to say you do it without complaining, without raising your employer's awareness and without working towards change, but teachers have to accept that there are some things that they have no control over and that if they want to do the best thing for their students they've got to accept and do the best that they can in implementing it [standardized testing].
>
> (Pam)

Here, the invitation for teachers to engage with policy is confined to its implementation and consumption, which is not exactly an engaging bid for their 'souls' (Ball 1999). As Pam noted: '. . . if we believe what we do, educationally and philosophically, about education, the Grade 7 test par- ticularly . . . goes against everything that we believe. And OK, so that's the policy, but I don't believe in it.'

The discourse of 'provider capture' (Lauder 1991) grants political legi- timacy for such containment; teachers, like professionals generally, are characterized as self-interested and unaccountable, particularly given the recent marketization of education.[3] In other words, teacher expertise is deemed to be suspect in the education marketplace and needs to be kept under surveillance (see Chapters 4 and 5); standardized testing regimes provide the quintessential example of these surveillance mechanisms, ostens- ibly focused on students' achievements but more cogently understood as coercively redirecting and re-evaluating teachers' and school practices. So, in evaluating students' test results, 'some teachers feel as if that then could be used to assess their own abilities as well' (Pam). This might not be how teachers themselves explain students' results but in the current context of schooling, influenced by neoliberal and neoconservative politics, 'I think it's interpreted like that by at least principals in schools and parents' (Pam).

The possibility of confining teachers' influence to contexts of policy practice also relies on a particular theoretical understanding and political employment of policy processes, as linear and discrete. In this account, policy implementation follows policy production and 'never the twain shall meet'. Again, this view of the policy process is not uncommon among teachers themselves:

> . . . a policy comes out. It goes through the Senior Policy Officer who sends it out for review at district level through the people in District Office. It comes to the principal who then puts it into practice in their school . . . In a high school, that starts with the principal and deputy, and then it's a HOD's [Head of Department's] job . . . before it gets to a classroom teacher.
>
> (Pam)

But 'educational reforms eventually have to work through teachers, and worthwhile reforms have to work *with* them' (Connell 1993: 57, emphasis added). In practice, policy is a far messier affair than the instrumentalism of 'steering at a distance' suggests. Schools are not passive recipients of state-determined directives, nor are teachers simply enablers of policy developed elsewhere (Ball 1990; Lingard and Garrick 1997). As we argue below, many teachers understand that how they think and what they do can make a difference to their students' education and life chances. Yet, this does not mean that they can do as they please, politically or theoretically. To believe this, despite the constraints of policy produced elsewhere, amounts to little more than 'naive optimism' (Shor and Freire 1987: 130) or 'romantic localism' (Troyna and Vincent 1995: 155).[4] Neither is resignation to the demands of policy a necessary response by teachers. As a teacher,

> . . . you don't have to be dominated by policy on assessment . . . but some people don't work it to its full extent . . . I've been in schools where [practice] is very regimented and follows very strict guidelines that match very much the original policy document. Then I've been in schools like ours where you can really twist it so that there's a lot of leeway.
>
> (Pam)

For teachers to engage with policy involves 'a politics of translation and negotiation' (Deever 1996: 256), or what de Certeau (1984) calls 'uses' and 'tactics': ways of making policy in contexts of practice and contexts of outcomes. It is to a consideration of these possibilities that we now turn.

The possibility of teachers' engagement with policy making

Influenced by cultural studies and particularly by the work of Michel Foucault, contemporary definitions in the policy sociology literature describe policy as text and as discourse (see, for example, Ball 1994a; Gale 1999b). Regarding the first, Ball argues that policy texts are physical codes: 'cannibalised products' (Ball 1994a) that carry meanings representative of the struggle and conflict of their production. According to Ball, once these meanings are captured in policy documents they become the focus of 'secondary adjustment' (Riseborough 1992), at times similarly 'disruptive' of meanings as the process of policy production itself, through various 'interpretations of interpretations' (Rizvi and Kemmis 1987) or 'refraction' (Prosser 1981; Freeland 1986). While there is recognition that policy texts are themselves political acts or 'textual interventions into practice' (Ball 1994a: 18), Ball also points out that they *'enter* rather than simply change power relations' (1994a: 20, original emphasis). In other words, policy texts are both products and tools of production where 'the translation of the crude, abstract simplicities of policy texts into interactive and sustainable practices of some sort involves productive thought, invention and adaptation' (Ball 1994a: 19).

Second, describing policy as discourse accounts for the politics of policy text production: 'what can be said, and thought, but also . . . who can speak, when, where and with what authority' (Ball 1994a: 21). Ball argues that policy discourses are *'ways* of talking about and conceptualizing policy' (Ball 1994b: 109, emphasis added), which are also 'practices that systematically form the objects of which they speak . . . [they] are not about objects; they do not identify objects, they constitute them and in the practice of doing so conceal their own invention' (Foucault 1972: 49). In short, policy discourse is like a double-hinged door; it is both productive of 'text' (understood broadly) and interpretive of it and, within this process, discourse informs textual writings *and* readings, including the latter's 'writerly' and 'readerly' possibilities (Gale 1999b). With respect to such possibility, discourses encode and decode policy texts in ways that constrain (and enable) their meanings and 'establish "discursive limitations"' (Henry 1993: 102) on policy outcomes. Hence, discourses do not simply assign meanings to texts in isolation but weave them together to form contexts. In the process, only some texts are included (named) and even then they are ordered and emphasized (framed) in distinctive ways, giving them meaning that they might not have in other contexts. Any one policy text, then, takes its meaning from its relationship – its relative positioning and emphasis – with other texts (its context) and from how these are discursively 'storied' (Gale 1994).

This is the current orthodoxy in the policy sociology literature, far more theoretically nuanced, cognizant of and explicit about (undemocratic) power relations in policy making than the 'rational' formulation/implementation accounts referred to above. And yet it does not seem to go far enough theoretically or empirically in helping teachers, for example, to engage in the policy process. In this text/discourse account, teachers, students and parents often seem to remain recipients or implementers of education policy not strictly producers of it, no matter how much we might acknowledge their ability to reinterpret. In other words, while 'policy as text' and 'policy as discourse' provide better answers to critical questions of 'what is really going on?', they do less well in answering 'what can we do about it?'. De Certeau (1984) provides a similar critique of Foucault's *Discipline and Punish* (1977): that Foucault's analysis of discipline focused on the 'microphysics of power' but he approached this from the perspective of the producers of discipline, not how these discipline regimes could be challenged and/or changed. Policy sociology, then, which draws on a similar Foucauldian analysis, could be subject to similar critique. If this is the case, what can be done about teachers' and others' exclusion from contexts of policy making becomes a matter of revisiting what is really going on, from the perspective of those whom policy affects. Borrowing from de Certeau (1984), this entails developing an understanding of teachers' participation in the policy process as tactical engagement. Such a project also serves our critical inquiry on two fronts: 'once one understands what tactics are, in de Certeau's sense, and appreciates their existential, cultural and political significance in relation to Production and Consumption, it becomes easier to recognize and build upon them' (Lankshear 2002: 17).

Briefly, then – to extrapolate from de Certeau (1984) and others who utilize and develop his work – from the perspective of policy *consumers*, policy is typically produced with the intention of turning 'spaces' (*of* learning, for example) into *producer* 'dominated spaces' (Lefevbre, in Lankshear 2002) or 'places' (*for* learning, such as schools), that is, to institutionalize them (Buchanan 1993, in Lankshear 2002). That much is already clear in the policy literature. However, drawing on de Certeau's work, we could also speculate that consumers who must occupy these places effectively become quasi-producers when they engage in tactics to subvert policy and/or put policy to use for intentions that its producers did not necessarily intend. This too is clear to policy sociologists, although less clarity tends to be offered on how this is done and, among those that approach this, few seem to theorize consumers' contributions in positive terms. The ability to reinterpret policy, often by gatekeepers, is about as far as discursive accounts seem to extend. Teachers' policy interpretations remain secondary, disruptive, refractive, adjustive, even cannibalized but never quite or fully productive;[5] indeed, policy interpretation frustrates and attempts to negate production. There is also the notion of subversion in de Certeau's account but this is understood as consumers being clever, creative, almost playful at times, as in a 'guileful ruse' (de Certeau 1984: 37).

In this more productive sense, de Certeau's work (or at least Lankshear's development of it) also raises the possibility for consumers to convert places into 'appropriated' spaces (Buchanan 1993, in Lankshear 2002) and democratize them, since tactics and uses 'are things that have the capacity to resist and subvert, to prey upon, spoof and exploit, and – *en masse* – to gradually

wear away at the world according to those whom de Certeau calls "Producers"' (Lankshear 2002: 1, emphasis added). As implied above, de Certeau
understands producers as those who dominate spaces – which become places,
once dominated – whereas consumers are those who occupy them. But just
as 'producers in one context are to some extent consumers in others'
(Lankshear 2002: 3), so too there seems the possibility for consumers to
negotiate spaces to contribute as policy producers and so make them their
own places. For Lankshear, 'this *has* to be a democratic pedagogical bottom line' (2002: 16, original emphasis), not simply because 'the people' are
involved *en masse*. That is, Lankshear's emphasis is a plea to struggle for a
democratic politics, rather than seeing it as a necessary empirical outcome.
To critically engage in uses and tactics in radical democratic ways, then, is
'to transform antidiscipline into permanent counterdiscipline' (Lankshear
2002: 16) or anti-hegemony into counter-hegemony (Connell 1993). As we
suggest in Chapter 5, there is no democratic intent in simply replacing one
form of arrogance with another.

Pam's engagements with standardized testing policy, which follow, are
not entirely of this subversive order; that is, they are not entirely tactical or
useful in an alternative sense. However, we have endeavoured to read her
account in 'readerly' ways that might be suggestive of tactics and alternative
uses available to teachers engaging with standardized testing policy. At times
we read 'against' Pam's comments to find tactics and uses to 'subvert' policy[6]
and, at least for this reason, our representations of these tactics and uses
should not be seen as comprehensive but as possible illustrations for others
'to recognize and build upon them' (Lankshear 2002: 17). Nevertheless,
Chapter 4, explores these conceptions of strategies (typically the preserve of
producers) and tactics (the resort of consumers) in the context of the social,
political and economic conditions that now confront educational leaders, in
ways consistent with a radical democracy. In this it is more strategic, promoting a democratic political activism, whereas our account in this chapter
is more tactical. We begin, then, with a consideration of tactics and then
of policy uses, as revealed by Pam in her account of teachers' responses to
standardized testing.

Policy making: tactics

Tactics in contexts of policy production are about making the most of one's
opportunities, of spaces: 'vigilantly mak[ing] use of cracks that particular
conjunctions open in the surveillance of proprietary powers. It poaches
them. It creates surprises in them' (de Certeau 1984: 37). In this account,
there are at least three ways in which consumers can tactically engage
with policy: one is to 'make do' with policy, to find creative ways to live
with it (the inventiveness that de Certeau refers to as 'bricolage'), another
is to try to 'put one over' policy, to 'wear away' at its weaknesses. And a
third, Lankshear's addition, engages a meta-analysis of policy that enables

consumers to recognize hegemony, in order not to be 'tricked' themselves. Each of these is evident in the tactics we have read into Pam's comments below (and also in the 'uses' that follow). In each case the tactic is presented in italics.

Standardized testing addresses something good teachers have always done. This is a tactic for 'making do', which, in this situation, makes standardized testing policy seem more palatable. It draws on the cultural history of schooling in a rough kind of way. If we were to rephrase Pam's comments from a tactical point of view, she might say 'Well, testing is not new to good teaching. I already know about how that can work to assist students. I plan on putting that knowledge to work.' While this disposition becomes clearer further below, what she actually said was:

> I believe that if you're doing your job well in Grade 1, 2 and 3, this [profiling of students' abilities] should have been occurring . . . By doing the Grade 2 test they have forced teachers to operate in classrooms using good practice . . . If you were in schools that were doing it well, they were always doing it [profiling students' abilities].

Standardized testing is just one aspect of what teachers do. Whereas the tactic above is mindful of an historical teaching context, the following interview excerpt is cognizant of a more contemporary one. Again, it illustrates a tactic of making do: incorporating standardized testing into what is already done, seeing it in the context of good teaching and learning. Here Pam explains how and why she found a way to use her own pedagogical expertise to satisfy the mandated testing requirement while teaching the 'normal' curriculum:

> It's not the only data gathering device – this one method of data gathering. Teachers rely on others as well . . . you build mandated standardized tests within your framework, into what you're doing in your programme, *so you don't have to work outside of it. The tests become an integral part of what you're doing* . . . really it's the [curriculum] elements that are guiding where you're going . . . [After all] it's a standardized test. You know ahead [of time] what's going to be tested, so you need to look at the common elements and instead of teaching towards that test, you teach the elements so that the students could do any test that those elements appear in . . . we always do very well in the test. And yet, our kids aren't any better academically than anywhere else in the state but because we address those common elements . . . So you don't have to say, 'All I'm doing is teaching towards the test' . . . 'How will I embed that into my normal teaching and programming, so that they're exposed to it and get practice?' Why teach towards that test? It defeats the purpose of testing, I feel.
>
> (Pam, emphasis added)

Standardized testing is only one way of assessing students' academic abilities. As the above two examples suggest, a common element in tactics are their appeal to spaces not under the discipline of policy. The meta-analysis that Pam employs in the following extract is of this order. Here she illustrates that she is not fooled by the spurious claims of standardized testing to be able to provide genuine indications of students' abilities. It is a tactic, however, that requires teachers to be good at what they do in order to be able to talk back to policy, to mobilize, to be a policy activist. In Pam's own words:

> . . . I'm also advocating that we don't just have assessment that's a once-off like an exam or an assignment   that we use observation and these tracking devices to keep a profile. We're profiling kids from Grade 8 to Grade 12 . . . instead of having Grade 5 and Grade 7 testing, there should be a better means of benchmarking them. But we haven't done that . . . [we need] strategies for improving student outcomes so they're not linked to the testing or anything like that. And I think as soon as we get away from linking it anyway with the testing, [the better off students and teachers will be].
>
> (Pam)

Standardized testing is only one way available to students to achieve academic success. 'Putting one over' policy is a tactic that realizes achievements which 'reading between the lines' of policy might suggest is not possible. The colloquialism, 'there is more than one way to skin a cat', is probably a good description of the tactician's stance in this regard. In this case, Pam tutors her students in the value of such tactics, pointing out to them that getting into university, one indicator of student achievement, is not solely dependent on doing well on standardized tests: 'Ever since I've arrived, I've told the kids, "this [test] is just one way of doing things. If you flunk out and do poorly, there are other means of getting into university."'

Policy: making uses

To put policy to uses other than those intended by its producers is to transcend the limits of place: to rename and/or reframe it, to reclaim spaces for teachers, students, parents and others. We might describe this engagement with policy as subversion 'from within . . . by many different ways of using them [policies] in the service of rules, customs or convictions foreign to the colonization which they [policy consumers] could not escape' (de Certeau 1984: 32). We see this as tantamount to naming elements in policy not originally included or acknowledged, to give it a plurality. Whereas 'tactics' are on the look-out for policy *opportunities*, 'uses' are sensitive to policy *possibilities*. In Pam's account, the latter enables teachers to 'put this particular assessment item, if it is an assessment item, in a broader context of other possibilities'. Again, in italics below are the possible uses for standardized testing policy that Pam envisages.

The unintended consequences of standardized testing can be used to argue for its demise. As a type of policy use, this is not unlike the meta-analysis, the 'smartness' (Lankshear 2002), employed above. It differs as use, however, in that it operates within the parameters of policy itself. Here Pam takes advantage of what is already known about standardized testing – that it has little validity with nonstandard students – and acts on this in ways that resist what was originally handed to her: an isolated assessment item. It is this internal validity of the policy that is called into question, on the basis that it does not take into account students' context-dependent development. What is also smart is the way she uses an unintended outcome of the policy, wasted resources, to argue for its demise:

> . . . I'm just concerned that they use a level thing that's [applied] right across the state. They use the same piece of assessment, and yet we all know that learning difficulties and disabilities are so different for everybody . . . [If] you come from [this area], it takes till about Grade 3 or Grade 4 to make up for the deficit that they've experienced, particularly in regard to exposure to books etc. . . . so your data in Grade 2 isn't really good data anyway. Some of these kids haven't been to preschool, and yet they operate the same regime [of testing] right through the state. They don't say, 'Well, we might do this [test] in Grade 3 at this school [instead of Grade 2]' . . . often, though, those kids don't need those resources. They just needed a bit of extra time. So we've whacked in a lot of money and the kids aren't ready anyway and it doesn't have a lot of impact on their ability. And if you look at some of the results of the Grade 2 test, some places where they've piled in that resource, it brings no results. It was just an age thing or a context thing that more resources won't do anything.
>
> (Pam)

Standardized testing can be used as a way of distributing and accessing resources. The alternative use for policy here can be likened to 'playing the system' or 'putting one over' policy producers who have other things in mind for policy. Standardized testing, for example, claims to be concerned about raising student achievement. But, as Pam explains:

> . . . if you really read the policy and if you look at the outcomes . . . what it does is identify kids who need extra support. And so if you look at it from a policy point of view, it's saying we're going to pick up these kids so that they don't slip through the net and use this method of identifying them, and so you can't get away from assessing them. It's a data gathering device to identify kids and when they've identified what happens, *and that's the resourcing.* So, to me, the Grade 2 test is not an assessment item, it's a data gathering device to allocate resources to allow these kids to 'value-add', if you want to call it that, to reach a benchmark.
>
> (Pam)

Given this reading of policy, many principals utilize standardized testing policy as a way of accessing resources for their schools, hence thwarting its stated intent. So, 'if you talk to principals, they'll say, "Oh, God, I'm going to lose X amount of dollars because we've just shown up as doing really well"' (Pam).

Standardized testing can be used to organize students into manageable groups and promote the interests of government. Principals, just like politicians, are adept at using policy to achieve particular political ends. Sometimes in the process they also seek to use it for ends that are not stated and/or were not intended by policy producers. The first of these is more akin to 'making do' while the second suggests 'putting one over'. Both of these uses are illustrated in Pam's observation:

> It's an assessment instrument, in a way, to give the state data to say these are the results of these kids when they're in Grade 7 . . . most schools don't use that data other than just to put them into 8A, 8B, 8C . . . if that. I think it's political, and each government uses that data for its own intent. For example, if the government wants to say, 'All the money we've put into primary school is valuable . . . In Grade 2, we identified these kids who needed support. We poured so many million dollars in and at Grade 5 this is the outcome. Look what we've done, how wonderful it is.'
>
> (Pam)

Conclusion

We have argued in this chapter that those who produce education policy, the *who* of policy production, tend to be removed from contexts of practice: 'Producers, by definition, are less directly acquainted with the responses of Consumers, and are too involved in Producing for the option of looking at Consumer operations to be seriously "available" to them' (Lankshear 2002: 3). Implied in this is that teachers (as well as students and parents) tend to be excluded from policy production. Instead, 'Producers include governments, urban planners, corporations, professional associations, legislatures, private utilities companies, scholarly and academic leaders, executives, and so on' (Lankshear 2002: 3). Policy sociology has not altered very much this traditional listing of 'who's who' in policy production, although it has revealed its elitist character and the hierarchical power relations invested in policy-making processes. In conjunction with this, cognizance of discourse has also delivered a more theoretically and politically informed rendition of *how* policy is produced; typically, through the strategies of dominant elites with some marginal concessions to policy actors 'on the ground'. While largely convinced by such explanation, our critique has been that this does not go very far in redressing teachers' negative positioning in the policy making process. In short, it offers a policy analysis *of* teachers rather than a policy analysis *for* them (Gordon *et al.* 1977; Kenway 1990), which raises questions about from which locations such analyses are best conducted (see Table 3.1). To draw on the space/place distinction above, understanding policy as text and as discourse seems to provide little space for teachers to engage in productive activities, even though we might recognize theoretically and empirically that they are capable of these.

The critical challenge is to produce a theory and a polity that can do this: reposition teachers (and others) as policy producers. As Lankshear counsels, 'under contemporary conditions, when the grid of discipline is "everywhere becoming clearer and more extensive", it becomes increasingly urgent to explore "how an entire society resists being reduced to it"' (2002: 2). We think that de Certeau's (1984) notions of uses and tactics may offer such possibilities, which goes against the grain of much policy work:[7] '... theorists often see strategy and tactics as oppositional terms, and thereby assume that de Certeau's approach belongs to a weaker category of resistance ... [but] tactics "define the limits of strategy" and force "the strategic to respond to the tactical" [Buchanan 1993]. Hence, tactics contain an active as well as a reactive dimension.' (Lankshear 2002: 7).

Lankshear's development of de Certeau's ideas, particularly shifting the intent of subversion from antidiscipline to counterdiscipline, adds two further dimensions to this account. First, it opens the door to a much more positive engagement with policy by teachers, to become *productive* contributors, not simply represented as reactive and negative and not simply consumers – our own development of Lankshear's position. Second, it requires a collective productivity, in keeping with a radical democratic intent. If policy consumers are to make the shift to being producers, it must be done *en masse* and gradually. But for the shift to aspire to a democratic process, it will also entail a different kind of producer: one who is not alienated by the policy-making process. This is the kind of political activist we described in Chapter 1 and to which we return in Chapters 4 and 5.

Our intent in this chapter has been to envisage greater scope for participation in the policy-making process by those located in contexts of practice, including teachers, students and parents. While policy production, like production in an economic sense, is not usually seen by ordinary folk as something that could or should be democratized, we want teachers in particular to think about what educational policy could and should be and be involved in its making. This is because we believe policy will be richer, more democratic and more effective to the extent that people 'on the ground' participate; policy can also then take advantage of their practical and theoretical knowledge. In brief, teachers, students, parents and others in the community need to be included in the production of policy, not just left to resort to the tactics of consumers in order to participate. It is to a consideration of such possibilities that we devote the following chapters.

Questions for discussion/research

- How can teachers critically engage students in high-stakes standardized taking?

- Why would the test-taking situation be experienced differently by majority and minority students?
- How can teachers discover tactics students employ to *survive* school and then use this knowledge to help students *succeed* in school?
- What steps can teachers take to have more of a collective voice in the making of educational policy?

Suggested readings

Ball, S. (1994) *Education Reform: A Critical and Post-structural Approach*. Buckingham: Open University Press, Chapter 4.

Ball, S. (1997) Policy sociology and critical social research: a personal view of recent education policy and policy research, *British Educational Research Journal*, 23(1): 257–74.

Gale, T. (1999) Policy trajectories: treading the discursive path of policy analysis, *Discourse: Studies in the Cultural Politics of Education*, 20(3): 393–407.

Hancock, L. (ed.) (1999) *Women, Public Policy and the State*. London: MacMillan, Chapter 12.

Trowler, P. (1998) *Education Policy: A Policy Sociology Approach*. East Sussex, UK: Gildredge Press, Chapter 3.

Yeatman, A. (ed.) (1998) *Activism and the Policy Process*. St Leonards, NSW: Allen & Unwin, Chapter 1.

four

Leadership: taking a radical democratic stance

This chapter seeks to identify the particular economic and social conditions confronting leaders in education and to set out the strategies and tactics they might utilize to respond to these conditions. Specifically, we suggest that education leaders are currently faced with changing bases of social cohesion, changing instruments of (economic) control and changing forms of organization. Informed by these changing conditions and by a radical view of democracy (Lummis 1996), we make a case for educational leadership that is characterized by distinctive democratic directions and influences. In particular, we argue that democratic leaders are those that enable the formation of social, learning and culturally responsive public educational institutions, in part by enabling contextually specific struggles to determine what is needed and by developing a politically informed commitment to justice for all.

In advocating a democratic approach for leaders, we are mindful that the field of leadership, including the more specific area of educational leadership, is replete with numerous and often contradictory views regarding its nature and merits. Cognizant of this history, and in endeavouring to make sense of the vast array of approaches to leadership, Leithwood *et al.* observe that each 'developed in a context of organizational and broader social goals, needs, norms, ideas, and expectations, which allowed one or several approaches to leadership to dominate, as an ideal, until such time as that context changed sufficiently as to more clearly favour yet another approach or approaches' (1999: 22–3).

Claimed here is a role for context in the determination of relevant approaches to leadership. On one level, Leithwood *et al.* (1999) argue that particular conditions, often reflected in commonly agreed goals, needs, norms, ideals and so on, influence the kinds of educational leadership that are seen as most appropriate at any one time. On another level, and perhaps less obvious in the above comments, these agreements or 'temporary settlements' (Gale 1999b) are also the subject of a micro politics of influence. Put simply, specific and general conditions change over time but these do not by themselves determine the dominance of one approach to educational leadership over another. Such determinations are the work of individuals and groups who exert dominance in any one historical moment and whose preferred approach to educational leadership is informed by their particular interests and their reading of and interaction with prevailing conditions. Finally, any one particular approach is not the same in every educational institution. That is, approaches to educational leadership are variously interpreted and attract various responses.

We begin in this way to make problematic the notion of leadership, to acknowledge its many antecedents and competitors, and that any new understanding must compete with these if it is to occupy the minds of current leaders in education. Drawing attention to educational leadership's history of shifting policy responses and contexts justifies the need for another look at how to conceive of educational leadership in contemporary times. This is because education leaders now face conflicting pressures, at one level to privilege some groups over others and, on another, to ensure that disadvantaged groups have a voice in educational decision making. Highlighting education leadership's history also represents a way of engaging with political determinations regarding how these leaders can and should respond to changed and changing conditions. Our intention is also to contribute to expanding the discussion on leadership beyond its sometimes-preoccupied interest in the individual qualities of leaders and to consider possibilities for supporting more collective actions and interests. Specifically, we see the potential for these interests to be addressed through a democratization of leadership.

Guiding questions/issues

Informed by Bourdieu and Wacquant, we conceive of educational leadership as a field that 'involves three necessary and internally connected moments' (1992: 104). The first of these draws attention to relations between a particular field (in this case, educational leadership) and broader 'fields of power'. In what follows, we rehearse accounts from Chapter 2 of these broader fields, particularly as they reveal: (1) the bases for social cohesion; (2) instruments of (economic) control; and (3) forms of organization evident in contemporary times; all matters pertinent to (educational) leadership. A second dimension of field analysis encompasses the 'field of positions'. Much of the leadership literature has focused (often narrowly) on these field positions: on designated leaders (principals and head teachers, for example), sometimes on 'followers' and on what are seen as their legitimate interrelations. Here, however, we avoid an explicit and singular account of these positions and relations, partly because of space but also because of the proliferation of such accounts within the literature. This is not to suggest that there remains no fruitful work to be done in relation to these matters. Rather, our intention is to explore connections Bourdieu sees between field positions and a third field of *stances*. Indeed, Bourdieu understands positions and stances as 'translations of the same sentence' (Bourdieu and Wacquant

1992: 105), combinations we have also referred to as 'vocality' (see Chapter 1 and also Gale 1997). It is this emphasis on stances, specifically taking a democratic stance on educational leadership, that occupies the interests of the second section of this chapter and, reflecting our socially critical disposition, which seeks to more explicitly address 'what can leaders do?' We begin, though, with a brief account of what currently faces educational leaders in broader fields of power. Indeed, this is the first thing to be done: to gain an appreciation for the prevailing conditions.

With what are we faced?

In the introductory essay to their most recent reader on the sociology of education, Brown *et al.* characterize 'the economic, cultural and social transformation' of modern societies in terms of the displacement of prosperity, security and opportunity by productivity, flexibility and choice; changes 'variously described as a shift from industrial to post-industrial, modern to post-modern and Fordist to post-Fordist' (1997: 1). Others account for these changes in the general settings of social life as revolutions in capital accumulation (Jameson 1983), information (Lyotard 1984) and image (Baudrillard 1981). In this first section we briefly outline the central features of these changes, particularly those that relate more closely to educational leadership. In Brown *et al.*'s view, these are evident in three broad and interrelated challenges. Specifically:

> The power of the nation state is threatened by the development of a global economy which has removed some of the key instruments used to control the economic destiny of nations. Bureaucracy, the form of organization which delivered mass education and industrial efficiency, is now considered outmoded and inefficient; while the notion of a common culture as the basis for social solidarity is being challenged by various groups asserting the right to educate their children according to their specific religious and cultural values.
>
> (Brown *et al.* 1997: 1)

We deal with the last of these first, namely, issues related to social cohesion and the search for ways in which to understand our individual and collective selves. We then consider contemporary instruments of economic and social control and, finally, contemporary forms of organization. In raising these as central concerns, we hasten to add two caveats. The first is to reiterate that these features of contemporary times are not intrinsically separate but are intimately related and mutually influential. They are dealt with separately here for analytical purposes, although effort is made to reveal their complexities as categories. Second, amid all this talk of change, some things seem to have stayed the same. That is, there are continuities as well as discontinuities in these explanations of contemporary times and the things that are different are not necessarily experienced in the same ways. Whitty *et al.*'s assessment is also that 'the similarities seem as striking as the discontinuities' (1998: 42). These are matters to keep in mind for the discussion on democratic leadership that follows; in other words, there are potential cracks for education leaders to exploit (see Chapter 3). In brief, while there is evidence of economic and social change, previous understandings and commitments potentially have elements to contribute to approaching contemporary times, albeit subject to some assessment and adjustment.

Changing bases for social cohesion

Increasingly, although not uniformly, societies are struggling over the degree to which they are homogeneous, what this means in today's world and the significance of the answers to these questions. Many countries are beginning to understand themselves as heterogeneous: without a single or common culture by which they can be identified and which might inform their social solidarity. For some, this is a frightening prospect. For others, it is cause for celebration, given an accompanying 'new rhetoric of legitimation' (Whitty *et al.* 1998: 42) for social difference. Under such influence, multiculturalism has largely become 'mainstream'. For more critical observers, however, the politics of recognition is more complex (Gale and Densmore 2000: 108–42). For example, they point to the situation that more women now enter the workforce yet their employment tends to be in service industries and characterized by insecurity of tenure (casual contract work, for instance). Similarly, access to university has reached mass proportions (Trow 1974), yet the financial distance between rich and poor – which more education (and credentials) was supposed to redress – is actually widening. Further, poverty is increasingly identified by gender (that is, particularly for women) and race (particularly people of colour) and is taking on a more definite geographical character with some population areas designated as 'the poor part of town' with reduced services and ageing infrastructure. Of similar concern are the disproportionately high numbers of incarcerated young black males and the high incidence of suicide amongst young males of all races (in Australia, particularly those youth located in regional areas).

At the same time, the almost worldwide introduction of new technologies and the globalization of national economies have tended to emphasize similarities and overlap amongst peoples. Economic and social relationships are no longer simply bounded by geography. Modes of production are increasingly global and mobile, as is employment. Multinational companies span previously 'walled' economies and the prospect of these companies shifting to more financially conducive regions provides challenges for local regulations and populations. Many employees, whose allegiances are invested in these large companies, now look to their employers for previously public services such as health care and, in some cases, education. On the latter, for example, some large companies are now in partnership with universities to provide degree programs for their employees. Companies may also be exhorted by governments to contribute to the common good by responsibly managing the environment. Other workers invest their futures in the share market. For example, the Australian and the United States populations have among the highest involvement in share ownership per person of any nation. The individualism of these markets has remarkably assimilating effects. What matters to many people becomes the profit their shares are making, irrespective of what the company may have to do to raise profits; for example, pollute the environment, lay off workers, exploit workers in third world countries and so on. Further, previously separate nations are banding together to form economic and social alliances; the European Economic Union and its unified currency (the Euro) providing just one example.

What do these things tell us about the prospects for or the nature of social cohesion in today's world? First, contemporary times are difficult to theorize. We need to be sensitive to both the range of local options and experiences available to people as well as shared (global, macro) experiences. According to Whitty *et al.*, 'to regard the current espousal of heterogeneity, pluralism and local narrative as indicative of a new social order may be to mistake phenomenal forms for structural relations' (1998: 42). In a similar manner, Ball distinguishes between first and second order effects: 'First order effects are changes in practice or structure (which are evident in particular sites and across the system as a whole), and second order effects are the impact of these changes on patterns of social access, opportunity and social justice' (1994a: 25–6).

We may be witnessing changes to certain social practices but there is evidence to suggest that underlying patterns of disadvantage have not changed very much and, in some respects, they may be deepening. That is, the changes to social relations do not seem to be producing 'consequences or outcomes that matter' (Leithwood *et al.* 1999: 22). The values and purposes of public education remain divided while entrenched patterns of disadvantage and underachievement reveal the institutionalization of each. Schooling continues with its fundamental purpose of differentiation and social selection, limiting the numbers of students it is willing to educate, accepting high failure rates and thereby undermining the bases for social cohesion.

Second, the problems are serious and persistent but it is clear they are being experienced in ways that require new forms of analysis. For example, there is increasing recognition that various forms of discrimination, based on social attributes such as gender, race and class, are often interrelated. McCarthy's (1997) 'nonsynchronous theory' of race relations provides one example of theorists endeavouring to address these issues. Young's 'five faces of oppression' (1990: 40–62) – exploitation, marginalization, powerlessness, cultural imperialism and violence – provide another. This is work that needs to be continued. We need critical ways of understanding and addressing social differences that translate into positive changed material conditions for disadvantaged social groups. But the politics of doing this are also important. That is, *how* it is to be done is just as important as *what*.[1] 'Standpoint epistemology' provides a useful starting point while Connell's strategy 'to *generalize* the point of view of the disadvantaged rather than separate it off' (1993: 52, original emphasis) proposes a general framework for how these new understandings might make connections with others; indeed, how the 'mainstream' might be rechannelled. Fraser (1997: 203) also provides critical insights for understanding how we might proceed when she encourages us to distinguish between those differences that are 'artifacts of oppression' and should therefore be eliminated, those that should be universalized and those that should be simply enjoyed. In other words, 'the task is to integrate the egalitarian ideals of the redistributive paradigm with whatever is genuinely emancipatory in the paradigm of recognition' (Fraser 1997: 204).

Changing instruments of (economic) control

Contemporary societies are also characterized by the withdrawal of nation states from direct intervention into a range of previously public domains, many of which are now subsumed within the economic arena. Less government regulation of the market, as the ideal outcome of these changes is often described, has a preference for global economies rather than walled or nationalist economies. This is not to suggest there are now no controls, just that the legitimation for much state regulation has been withdrawn while those controls that are retained and others that have replaced them tend to be better hidden. Hence, many markets appear to be self-regulating; economies are now seen to be regulated more by markets (often ruled by self-interest and competitive individualism) than by nation states (potentially ruled by collective interests and mutual interaction). Some understand this as a 'withering' of the nation state (Dale 1992). Examples of this thinking can be seen in comments by American economists contemplating the possibility of an official interest-rate rise by Alan Greenspan (Governor of the United States Government's Federal Reserve Bank) and its likely effect on US share market prices. As one Credit Suisse economist commented: 'The Fed doesn't control the market. The Fed is like a cork that bobs up and down on the waves of the market' (Cable Network News, October 1999). While there has been a multiplication of nation states in recent times, it is also true that they survive on currency, energy, commerce and so on, from elsewhere. Transnational processes like the global market, science and technology are reshaping everything from 'autonomous' nation states to food products. These processes are ongoing; they are forming and reforming worldwide social relations. Their potential includes increasing the possibilities for forms of human cooperation and organization.

In globalized economies, nation states and their citizens have sought new competitive advantages. For many, education offers such possibilities and is conceived within much government policy and practice as central to a nation's economic prosperity. But what is enacted is a more micro-economic form of human capital, targeted at the education and training of select individuals rather than at macro societal benefits previously imagined within a Keynesian approach to policy (Marginson 1993, 1997). Individuals are now seen to derive significant and specific economic benefits from education, more so than their (host) nations, and are therefore increasingly obliged by governments to contribute to its financing (for example, through Australia's Higher Education Contribution Scheme). This is quite apart from their families' and their own more general contributions through the taxation system. More broadly, public education systems are regarded as careless consumers of government funds and are required to develop greater efficiencies in how such funds are expended. The marketization of education is seen as a way of resolving these problems, enabling the distribution of government funds (sometimes conceived in the form of vouchers) to specific individuals rather than to institutions, extracting funds (fees for service) directly from individual consumers and the transformation of education institutions into wholesalers and retailers of knowledge commodities; all contribute towards a shift from public to private responsibility (see Chapter 6). Nevertheless, private institutions of education still rely on significant government funding, although often in more subtle and veiled ways than their public counterparts.

Within government schooling systems, this shift in where responsibility resides is often referred to as devolution, albeit conceived within a distinctively neoliberal frame (Martin *et al.* 1994). Government schools are to be self-managing, yet while they have gained more responsibilities and are more closely accountable to their communities, authority is still primarily invested in other arenas. For example, system reporting requirements, account-keeping procedures, national curriculum documents and frameworks, standardized testing regimes and so on, all ensure that particular activities are pursued in schools rather than other activities; requirements that are not always cognizant of local needs, interests and conditions. This new collection of state regulations may appear less authoritarian compared to their forebears yet their effects are better described as 'steering at a distance' (Kickert 1991; Marceau 1993). Moreover, such controls have a certain market logic, given that education systems have been repositioned within society as suppliers of different kinds of workers required by the economy.

Capitalism today is driven by both globalization and the fragmentation of mass markets. The globalization of competition makes competition fierce. Gee *et al.* (1996) argue that this situation supports many more workers with the abilities to learn and adapt quickly, take responsibility and communicate to leaders what they need to know. Top-down controls have been recognized as not effective for achieving these goals; workers are encouraged to become 'empowered'. Responsibilities at work appear to be spread out more throughout an organization, although that has not been true for authority. Notions of strong management are often in tension with more professional or collective approaches to decision making in both the private and public sectors. Moreover, more workplaces today expect their employees to be loyal and committed to their place of work. This emotional commitment is expected even during economically risky times and even though the work-force is increasingly differentiated. On the latter:

> ... distinctions can now be made between the 'rising one-fifth', an elite minority capable of commanding the highest salaries, and the 'falling four-fifths', composed of a significant middle group destined to perform more routine and less well-remunerated tasks and a growing underclass experiencing periods of unemployment and very low-paid part-time or temporary work.
>
> (Helsby 1999: 4)

As Lyotard observes, 'the transmission of knowledge is ... designed to ... supply the system with players capable of acceptably fulfilling their roles at the pragmatic posts required by its institutions' (1984: 48). Such observations challenge neoliberal assumptions about education as primarily an individual benefit and challenge us to expand our understanding of the *public* purposes of learning (see Chapter 6). They also reflect a different positioning for individuals in society and a different role for education in general. According to Lyotard, the motivations today for acquiring knowledge are for profit and power. That is, the response to contemporary encounters with knowledge 'is no longer "Is it true?" but "What use is it?"' and even then this is taken to mean 'Is it saleable' and/or 'Is it efficient?' (Lyotard 1984: 51).[2] In short, despite some occasional rhetoric to the contrary, governments do not offer an emancipatory discourse of education. Moreover, no one is even certain that higher education gives a positive economic return to society at large. Credentialism, supposedly the 'guarantee' of worker productivity, keeps many potentially productive individuals out of the high-status, high-paying jobs while conferring even more resources on those who, because of their social class origins, gender and/or race, already possess relative power and prestige.[3] Even for the privileged, downsizing and restructuring policies are impacting on positional competition within the middle classes.

What, then, do these things tell us about (economic) controls in contemporary times? First, while the state appears more aloof from the economy and seems to be withdrawing the extent of its regulative function in other public domains, its contemporary set of controls ensure that it remains a significant player (Keating and Davis 2000). Second, many social and cultural areas have been reconceived in economic terms, particularly education which has been given a 'starring role' (Ball 1990). Third, the controls exerted on education are increasingly directed at individuals. While Henry (1992) has demonstrated the effectiveness of steering-at-a-distance strategies within the context of Australia's higher education system in the late 1980s and early 1990s – specifically how the government ensured the compliance of institutions with its reform agenda – Gore (1998), drawing on Foucault (1977), has shown how more individualized controlling mechanisms are increasingly at work within classrooms, in the form of strategies of surveillance, normalization, exclusion, classification, distribution, individualization, totalization and regulation. Similar accounts of micro control mechanisms in Australian higher education (Coady 2000; Gale and Densmore 2000) are also beginning to emerge in the USA.

Changing forms of organization

Most workers in western societies are now familiar with the managerial concept of restructuring and most teachers are familiar with how this is played out in schools in the form of school-based management, self-managing schools and the like. However, there often appears some discrepancy between the rhetoric accompanying these reforms and the evidence in real educational contexts. For example, contemporary management rhetoric advocates entrepreneurial (and 'flat') rather than bureaucratic (and hierarchical) forms of organization, rule making rather than rule following, and team and project work rather than fixed divisions of tasks. Yet in old bureaucracies and within many educational institutions, an important continuity seems to be the continued hierarchization of decision making, especially over the most substantive and critical issues. The absence of teachers in the policy-making process (see Chapter 3), for example, can be seen as part of their de-professionalization (see Chapter 5).

Such contradictions are highlighted in much critique of Caldwell and Spinks' (1988) account of self-managing schools, critique that questions the kinds of participation, the kinds of access to resources and the account of differences implied within their model (see Smyth 1993). For example, participation under the leadership Caldwell and Spinks describe is often characterized as 'contrived collegiality' (Hargreaves in Whitty *et al.* 1998: 58) and as 'a safe administrative simulation of collaboration' that is 'administratively regulated, compulsory, implementation-orientated, fixed in time and space and predictable' (Whitty *et al.* 1998: 58).

But it is not only teachers' participation that appears hollowed out. Leadership, too, is typically subservient to the requirements of an existing system:

> In many ways the concept of leadership has been chewed up and swallowed down by the needs of modern managerial theory. The idea of leadership as a transforming practice, as an empowerment of followers, and as a vehicle for social change has been taken, adapted and co-opted by managerial writers so that now leadership appears as a way of improving organizations, not of transforming our world. What essentially has happened is that the language of leadership has been translated into the needs of bureaucracy.
>
> (Foster 1989: 45)

One must question the value, then, of 'transformational' leadership as it is now utilized and understood; a leadership that in practice does not live up to the promises of its nomenclature. As Leithwood *et al.* explain: ' "to transform" is "to change completely or essentially in composition or

structure" . . . So any leadership with this effect may be labelled transformational, no matter what specific practices it entails or even whether the
changes wrought are desirable' (1999: 27).

What, then, do these things tell us about educational organizational arrangements in today's world? First, that a new conception of educational
leadership seems warranted, one that is not simply focused on change
without greater consideration of its potential (anti)democratic effects on
organizations. This is not to diminish the need for changed arrangements or
to suggest that we should 'go back' to some mythical golden past. Criticism
of a Caldwell and Spinks (1988) self-managing school is not necessarily a
call for a return to better times. Indeed, as Coady notes with respect to the
shortcomings of previous arrangements in higher education: 'We need not
think that there was a golden age of universities [or schooling] when the
ideal was realized fully or nearly so: the history of such institutions, as of
all institutions, abounds in corruption, unjustified privilege, mediocrity and
venality' (2000: 5).

Second, in a context where productivity, flexibility and choice are seen
as the new imperatives for educational organizations: 'academics are experiencing conditions which diminish their autonomy, including increasing
demands for accountability through mechanisms like "performance appraisal"
. . . at the very same time as workers in other industries are experiencing
conditions which require them to act more autonomously' (Taylor 1999:
75).

Again, here is evidence of first order changes to organizational arrangements without very much evidence of second order effects from these changes
(Ball 1994a). What are often referred to as 'new times' have indeed brought
changes in forms of organization but their effects can seem remarkably
similar and may not be very different.

What can leaders do?

In their critique of educational leadership approaches, Leithwood *et al.* assert
that 'principals typically do not employ political and symbolic frames in
the interpretation of their problems. Structural and human resource frames
alone shape their sense of what needs to be done in their schools' (1999:
22). One test for any new approach to educational leadership, then, is
whether it is cognizant of the contemporary political and symbolic frames
or 'fields of power' discussed above. This needs to be more than just a
distant awareness but neither should this become so overriding or dominant
in the minds of educational leaders that they themselves become instruments of power, unable to engage with possibilities and opportunities to
interact with and within these frames. Last century, John Dewey was concerned about 'the powerful influence of business standards and methods
in the community [and how this] affects the members of an educational
system', including its leaders. He also recognized that, at times, 'business

and other details are so pressing [on educational leaders] that connection with the intellectual and moral problems of education is had only at arms' length' (Dewey 1958: 68). We might similarly contemplate the influence of the market and contemporary forms of governance on today's educational systems and leaders.

In raising these matters, Dewey (1958: 68) was concerned to offer the educational leader a different perspective and to warn, 'it is important that his [sic] conception of the directly educational phase of his work be unified with his conception of the social relations of administration, both inside and outside the school.' In Bourdieu's terms (Bourdieu and Wacquant 1992), Dewey identifies here the interrelations between fields of power and positions. In this section, we pursue these connections within Bourdieu's field of stances and as the place to begin a new appreciation for educational leadership. We further argue that this field of stances encompasses what others see as the 'two basic attributes . . . common to many otherwise diverse, generic definitions of leadership' (Leithwood *et al.* 1999: 55), namely, direction setting and influence. They are attributes echoed in Dewey's observations that 'it is the main business of . . . the school to influence directly the formation and growth of attitudes and dispositions, emotional, intellectual and moral' (1958: 62).

In what follows, these issues of direction setting and influence are described respectively as enabling strategies and tactics (see Chapter 3). Dewey's intention in referring to such matters is primarily to emphasize the *educational* aspects of leadership. Here we want to assign a particular character to the strategies and tactics envisaged by Dewey's (1958) democratic vision for educational administration and by our own account of *democratic* educational leadership. Our intent is to suggest a direction for the transformation of schooling other than market-based initiatives. We speak of the need for educational leadership to be resourceful by being inclusive and to show initiative and courage in establishing equal opportunities for all students in the face of changing and challenging economic and social conditions. Hence, our intention is to challenge the market discourse that has enveloped education in recent times, a discourse that confronts the notion of failing schools and students in order to create genuine possibilities for more explicitly collective agendas that take account of difference in ways that are not simply reactive.

Enabling strategies

A first general stance adopted by democratic leaders finds expression in the enabling strategies they establish within their institutions. As imagined here, a democratic stance reflects a recognitive approach to social justice (Young 1990; Gale and Densmore 2000). This is a consciously normative definition of leadership that seeks to assist educational organizations in their: (1) self-identification and recognition; (2) self-expression and self-development; and

(3) self-determination and decision making – issues that parallel the central features identified above in contemporary economic and social conditions. Here 'self' is dialectically understood. That is, individuals do not exist in isolation but in relationship; hence Bourdieu's reference to them as social agents, 'the bearers of capitals' (Bourdieu and Wacquant 1992: 108). The group or organized 'self' is similarly a recipient of the distribution of capitals and implicated in their preservation and subversion. It is from such understandings that Dewey (1958: 69) encourages educators to consider, 'is it the social function of the school to perpetuate existing conditions or to take part in their transformation?' And it is from such an understanding of 'self' that we recognize this to be a question for school communities and the broader society in which it is located, not simply the principal. To put this another way, the intent of democratic leadership is to strategically establish the conditions for 'new' relationships (genuine expressions of interest, understanding and aspiration) and for 'new' actions (proactive engagements with local and global constraints and opportunities); their newness deriving as much from who is involved and how, as from an appreciation for changing economic and social conditions. Outlined below, then, are three strategies to enable more inclusive and dynamic organizations.

Enabling social organizations: stances on self-identification and recognition

Much management literature and practice is concerned with the development of mission statements, corporate visions, strategic plans and the like, as a way of establishing institutional and systemic directions, often imposed on their communities (including those impositions internal to the institution) and used for promotion within the marketplace. Self-identification, as understood here, is a much broader concept. It is concerned with the recognition of broader fields of power in the formation of who people are, how they see themselves and who they want to become. And it is more specifically concerned with ownership and respect, initiated through a mutuality of 'I'm prepared to listen'. It is motivated by aggressive encouragement and opportunities to understand one's identity historically and to use one's history self-critically. Self-determined identities are also more dynamic, growing and developing through interactions with other individuals and groups and within broader political and symbolic frames. Democratic leadership acknowledges that in contemporary societies, identity is created more than given. Further, the process of identity construction is ongoing, bringing with it uncertainty and ambiguity. While democratic leadership entails 'a definite idea of the place and function of the school in the ongoing processes of society, local and national' and requires 'a definite point of view, firmly and courageously adhered to in practice' (Dewey 1958: 68), it also allows for transition, variation and innovation. It is a self-identified view rather than one imposed by others.

This same stance can also be taken in relation to public schools, generating a differential public system in which schools can be distinctive; built, in part, from the ground up, strategically enabling people to develop their capacities to direct their own futures while supported by a shared framework and common purposes. It is this broader sense of leadership that has the potential to allow for diversity and responsiveness, for the development of individuals who recognize, value and work to critically enhance their connectedness to education institutions. In turn, democratic education is based, in large part, upon the real, non-school lives of their pupils and upon life outside of school, preparing students for life in the fullest sense.

At both local and global levels, what is envisaged is a sense of 'who *we* are' and 'what *we* want to achieve' as an educational enterprise, which is always a relational understanding dependent on a sense of others, their sense of themselves and our ties to one another. What are created are spaces for difference, for educational leadership to acknowledge race (Rizvi 1997), gender (Limerick and Lingard 1995) and social class (Yates 2000) and to challenge these when discrimination is experienced. In short, this stance on self-identification and recognition engages strategies directed at shared ownership, active trust, familiarity, mutuality, negotiated authority, genuine opportunities, courage and encouragement. They are strategies implicit in a 'democracy of emotions' (Giddens 1994: 16; Gale and Densmore 2000: 146) and enable progress toward more participatory and diverse modes of organization and forms of cooperation.

Enabling learning organizations: stances on self-expression and self-development

A second set of strategies is directed at the creation of forums for individuals' and groups' self-expression and self-development and 'in which the teaching corps takes an active and cooperative share in developing the plan of education' (Dewey 1958: 67). Dewey describes this as 'intellectual leadership', which takes the character 'of intellectual stimulation and direction, through give-and-take, not that of an aloof official imposing, authoritatively, educational ends and methods' (1958: 69).

By this account, the democratic leader 'treat[s] the school itself as a cooperative community' (Dewey 1958: 69). This necessitates: (1) establishing forums within which to hold important conversations, to promote individuals' development as well as group interests; (2) establishing multiple and diverse opportunities to express one's views; (3) establishing ways in which individual and group strengths and interests can be encouraged to develop; (4) embracing (new) technologies that will ensure generational, successional, transitional leadership and change; and (5) establishing critical friends and mentoring schemes amongst leaders, and potential leaders, including those from a school's communities, rather than supervision characterized by 'disciplinary power' (Foucault 1977).

A democratic stance in relation to self and group expression and self and group development, then, is evidenced in strategies that foster: conversational spaces; open interactions; available, flexible and adaptable opportunities; generosity; resourcefulness; modeling and mentoring; and planned transitions and successions – for all those involved in the educational project. They are strategies conducive for learning organizations (see Leithwood *et al.* 1999: 65–188) but also for developing 'a democracy of social space' (Gale and Densmore 2000: 148). The creation of schools as micro-communities, where students, teachers, parents and administrators exercise and develop their capacities to communicate and work with one another and others are central dimensions to these strategies. The locus of control over cooperation does not reside solely within the school, but instead retains the capacity for spontaneity, unpredictability and ongoing rich relationships with diverse constituencies. Ideas about the common good, about how public spaces reflect both individual and group interests and about the values of equality and fairness are also critiqued and nurtured.

Enabling responsive organizations: stances on participation and decision making

Democratic leadership is also concerned with meaningful participation, which necessarily gives all those involved substantial responsibility and the necessary flexibility to work together to make and implement serious and wide-ranging decisions. Participation should involve breadth as well as depth. Put simply, diverse others need to be involved, trusted and respected, particularly those whom the decisions will affect. This means strategically establishing collaborative relationships with a range of groups – professional associations, businesses, community-oriented programmes, progressive foundations, and so on – who have an interest in quality public education. Such widespread public participation in education is likely to lead to better decisions about what it really takes to achieve quality public education – for everyone – because they are based on common interests and common responsibilities, aimed at creating safe spaces in which school personnel and the wider community are free to envision, plan and experiment together.

In brief, a democratic stance toward participation and decision making involves engaging strategies that foreground respectful relationships, associations, consideration, reflexivity, consultation, empathy, active cooperation and community mobilization. They are strategies that serve culturally responsive organizations and 'a democracy of systems and routines' (Gale and Densmore 2000: 151).

Enabling tactics

These three sets of strategies directed at establishing social, learning and culturally responsive organizations, are not givens but need to be negotiated. Below we briefly outline six tactics informed by research into the production of Australian higher education policy (Gale 2001b, 2003) – trading, bargaining, arguing, stalling, manoeuvring and lobbying – as applied to issues of educational leadership. While their separations imply a certain discreteness, these tactics are more cogently understood as interrelated. For instance, a certain amount of stalling can be exercised in the process of bargaining, lobbying can involve a degree of trading and argument, while a tactical manoeuvre might involve several tactics of negotiation. It should be noted that they are not exclusively the preserve of democratic leaders, as conceived here. Rather, what is implied is that such leaders need to know how to utilize these tactics for democratic purposes, how to engage with them when utilized by others and how to instruct others in their use. Cognizant of these relations, each of the tactics is briefly explained.

Trading: negotiating the exchange of interests – Democratic leaders in education, in the sense described here, are traders. They are skilled at listening to different opinions and offering alternative points of view with the explicit aim of acknowledging that there are multiple ways to approach issues, problems and questions. All the while, leaders proceed from clear principles that promote socially and culturally sensitive practices and democratic accountability. In most public schools today, a genuine exchange of this sort presupposes an active commitment to increasing the representation of marginalized minority groups, the economically disenfranchised and those who have a first language other than English.

Bargaining: negotiating the moderation of interests – Democratic leaders in education are also adept at bargaining and maintaining open dialogue while they work toward creating institutional structures and cultures that affirm diversity. Their conversations distinguish different standpoints and different interests, including their implications for achieving shared goals and, when necessary, re-examining and renegotiating these goals.

Arguing: negotiating the persuasion of interests – There is an educative component to argumentative tactics of negotiation. Information can be used tactically, hence arguing involves more than just having the 'right' information. As Lyotard (1984: 51) explains, 'what is of utmost importance is the capacity to actualize the relevant data for solving a problem "here and now" and to organize that data into an efficient strategy.' Different conventions for arguing, for example, need to be understood, accepted and adopted when appropriate. Democratic leaders involve others in the exchange of ideas by equitably sharing accurate and sufficient information and by working collaboratively with diverse others to reach agreements.

Stalling: delaying the negotiation of interests – Others may possess skills of persuasion but choose not to employ them, instead preferring to delay their engagement with change. Depending on the situation, stalling can be a useful tactic for democratic leaders (Knight 1998). However, leaders are also confronted with stalling tactics when others use them. Their task becomes one of keeping the decision-making processes and conversations from stagnating while striving for equality of status among participants.

Manoeuvring: negotiating the circumvention of interests – Sometimes moving discussions forward may require democratic leaders to divert from intended paths and to explore other options until agreements, even if tentative, can be reached. Manoeuvrings of this kind can involve considerable interaction, especially when representatives of diverse communities try to speak in concert when modes of collective speech are broached.

Lobbying: negotiating the coalition of interests – Tactics of negotiation also entail establishing commonalities. Democratic leaders acknowledge the greater expertise of others, including that of nonprofessionals, in certain situations. They demonstrate their willingness to accept decisions that are genuine outcomes of democratic procedures within an overall context that prioritizes the eradication of inequalities in students' academic achievement, school financing and public participation in educational decision making.

Conclusion

We began this chapter with an account of the economic and social conditions now confronting educational leaders. While these conditions are potentially dangerous for societies and their education institutions and systems, there are also opportunities. Moreover, the dangers are not entirely new although in some cases they seem to have intensified. For example: 'practically nowhere do teachers' groups have the power to decide what the budget of their institution will be; all they can do is allocate the funds that are assigned to them, and only then as the last step in the process' (Lyotard 1984: 50).

As we have implied, we can resign ourselves to these problems or we can confront them: 'the more difficult demand may be cultivating and harnessing the willingness to embrace the kind of identity as an educator within which nurturing and employing [strategies and] tactics is not merely significant but is an *absolutely necessary* element' (Lankshear 2002: 17, original emphasis).

Educational leaders now face multiple and contradictory pressures that in many respects mirror the set of Chinese characters that symbolize the word 'crisis'. In grammatical terms, its Chinese representation is a compound word consisting of two characters, the first meaning danger and the second, opportunity.[4] Elsewhere crisis is described as 'settlements in waiting', as an inescapable element in temporary settlements, however well hidden or denied (Gale 1999b). The Chinese representation of crisis seems of a similar intent with danger and opportunity positioned in relation, although one is necessarily illustrated before the other. Even more clearly than the notion of temporary settlements is the way in which the juxtaposition of these characters addresses the two questions outlined above, namely, 'with what are we faced?' and 'what can leaders do?'.

Democratic educational leaders who take up this challenge engage strategies conducive to the development of social, learning and culturally responsive organizations and employ tactics directed at their achievement. Yet, in proffering these strategies and tactics we do not intend to imply that democratic leadership is mostly procedural and difference-neutral. Nor have we meant to imply that democratic leadership will look the same in all contexts, in all situations. Rather, the radical democratic leader necessarily enables particular conversations and struggles to determine what is needed, when, and how to get there in specific situations. This also is a process that needs to be acknowledged for presenting opportunities for *all* participants to develop a socially critical disposition and a commitment to radical democracy and justice for all, a theme we now extend to Chapter 5.

Questions for discussion/research

- How can principals act in democratic ways when faced with limited financial budgets and expanding teacher, student and community needs?
- How is a shared vision for schooling possible amongst teachers, students, parents and communities, which also acknowledges their differences?
- How much and what kinds of influence can principals exert and still engage in democratic leadership?

Suggested readings

Bell, J. and Harrison, B. (1998) *Leading People: Learning from People: Lessons from Education Professionals.* Buckingham: Open University Press, Chapter 3.

Bottery, M. (1992) *The Ethics of Educational Management: Personal, Social and Political Perspectives on School Organization.* London: Cassell, Chapter 12.

Lauder, H., Jamieson, I. and Wikeley, F. (1998) Models of Effective Schools: Limits and Capabilities, in Slee, R. and Weiner, G. with Tomlinson, S. (eds) *School Effectiveness for Whom? Challenges to the School Effectiveness and School Improvement Movements.* London: Falmer Press, Chapter 5, pp. 51–69.

Leithwood, K., Jantzi, D. and Steinbach, R. (1999) *Changing Leadership for Changing Times.* Buckingham: Open University Press, Chapter 8.

Professionalism: a framework for just social relations

In this chapter we explore different ways of thinking about the professionalism of teachers and teacher-educators. We begin with an overview of traditional understandings of what constitutes a professional. We then contrast this to teachers' and teacher-educators' actual work situations and practices, including ways in which the world of education is changing. Specifically, we discuss the rise of (sometimes contradictory) corporate and market interests as central organizing mechanisms currently at work upon and within schools and faculties of teacher education and how these are influencing teachers' and teacher-educators' work, including their ideas and ideals about their professionalism. We argue for the need to develop an alternative democratic persona and a context that increases educators' voices at all levels of educational decision making and which also engages their surrounding communities. Our underlying aim is to contribute to the development of ideas about how schooling and teacher education can better stimulate and draw upon educators' knowledges while at the same time challenge social inequalities.

Guiding questions/issues

Teachers and teacher-educators often make claims about being professionals and are frequently exhorted to higher levels of professionalism by their colleagues, administrators and various sectors of society. At one level, connections between 'profession' and 'teacher' are understandable given their origins in words such as 'profess' (from the Latin, to declare) and 'professor' (a teacher and/or one who claims to know). But what exactly does it mean to be a professional teacher? In particular:

- What reinforces the association of teacher professionalism with notions of superior status and privilege?
- Why do some teachers and teacher-educators feel that their professionalism is under threat given the current imperative for education to serve national economic interests?
- Does the notion of professionalism hinder or facilitate advancing the interests of the least advantaged?

These are the questions that direct our exploration of different ways of thinking about the professionalism of teachers, including teacher-educators. We begin with an overview of traditional understandings of what constitutes a professional. We then contrast this to teachers' and teacher-educators' actual work situations and practices, including ways in which the world of education is changing. Specifically, we discuss the rise of (sometimes contradictory) corporate and market interests as central organizing mechanisms currently at work upon and within schools and faculties of teacher education. We argue that these interests are influencing teachers' and teacher-educators' work, including their ideas and ideals about their aspirations, their purposes and their relationships with other groups in civil society.

Throughout, we note that much of the research and scholarship on professionalism, particularly as it relates to the broad field of teaching, demonstrates the need for an awareness of the concept's complexity. Specifically, we suggest that, as an ideology, traditional conceptions of professionalism restrict the possibilities for educators to work with parents, students and other community members – especially para- and 'non'professionals – in efforts to improve the quality of teaching and learning for students. In contrast, we argue for the need to develop more democratic practices that increase educators' voices at all levels of educational decision making and which also engage teachers' surrounding communities. Our underlying aim is to contribute to the development of ideas about how schooling and teacher education can better stimulate and draw upon educators' knowledges while at the same time challenge social inequalities.

The data we utilize – semi-structured interviews and observations – are illustrative rather than formative of the arguments we present and are derived from a larger corpus of research data broadly concerned with detailing a cultural economy of education, particularly in relation to democratic and socially just practices in schools; in this case, what this means for teachers' professionalism. Australian and United States sources of these data are referenced according to: (1) participants' positions, as student-teachers (ST), teachers (T) and teacher-educators (TE); and (2) number, to distinguish between those similarly positioned; thus: ST3, T5, TE1, and so on. We see this data not as secondary to the theoretical debates in which we engage but as representative of those debates and of the need for a forum in which they can be aired. We begin our discussion, then, with a traditional account and critique of professionals as those who 'know best'. This is followed by a discussion, again from a position of critique, of professionals as deserving recognition. We conclude with a call for teachers and teacher-educators to rethink how they might better work with their respective communities, especially with those groups which society has failed to serve. It is this third discussion that informs the professional framework we envisage for just social relations within and between schools and communities. Each of the three themes consists of two parts that provide different emphases on the theme in question.

We *know* best

The claims that educators traditionally have made about their professionalism are very similar to those in other occupational fields, particularly in the prestigious areas of law and medicine (Greenwood 1957; Wilensky 1964; Barber 1965; Bidwell 1965; Volmer and Mills 1966; Weick 1976; Saks 1983). In these accounts, professionals draw upon specialized knowledge in an environment that is free from interference, especially by nonprofessionals, and in ways that are in the best interests of those in their care: the classic combination of expert knowledge, autonomous judgements and ethical practice.

The first of these criteria, the possession of valuable knowledge – specialist knowledge that is not held by lay people – is probably the professionals' most significant claim and, in the main, informs their subsequent assertions for independence (discussed below). As one participant in our research put it, 'you've got to be knowledgeable, confident and competent' (T1) to be a professional teacher. Knowledge that counts most in this context is that which is associated with traditional academic agendas (Gale and Densmore 2000: 76–8). Briefly, this involves an epistemology valued and controlled by dominant cultural groups, typically abstract and theoretical in character and traditionally associated with a ruling elite. Given their relocation within universities, the professionalism of teacher-educators is informed at least in part by the particularities of this academic environment. Whereas some theorists account for the professionalization of teaching in terms of political advocacy, particularly that of teacher unions (Henry *et al.* 1988), Labaree (1992) argues that the teacher professionalization movement can, in large part, be traced back to the interactive developments of the professionalization of teacher-educators and the rise of a science of teaching. Seeking a remedy for their generally low status, teacher-educators began applying the methods of educational psychology to issues of teaching and learning.[1] The construction of a science of teaching within a rationalist worldview helped teacher-educators to secure status within university contexts. It became the paradigm around which they developed their careers, their competence and their understandings of the educative process (Labaree 1992: 143). The connections between knowledge and power in these settings help explain why teacher-educators have come relatively late to employ more context-bound, particularistic or interpretive accounts of teaching and to critique the scientific-rationalist model of research.

For many teachers and teacher-educators, their particular expertise includes specialized knowledge about a content area (such as mathematics, reading and so on) as well as knowledge about teaching and learning processes – how knowledge is passed on to and acquired by others – including understandings acquired through experience, observation and experimentation. Frequently, it is practical knowledge that is championed by teachers in schools whereas, as noted above, teacher-educators are often imagined as having a disposition for more theoretical interests in or approaches to teaching and learning. One student-teacher in our research clearly illustrated this perceived distinction between teachers and teacher-educators and the respective emphases of practice and theory that are seen to be embodied within them. While commenting on what it means to be a professional teacher, she noted, 'It means you go into the classroom and act like the normal classroom teacher should. You're not just there commenting from the sidelines' (ST1).

Some teacher-educators see their own distinctions between teachers' expertise in 'pedagogical knowledge' (of effective teaching and learning processes) and what Shulman (in Burbules 1997) refers to as 'pedagogical content knowledge' (not just knowledge about curricula but also an understanding of knowledge as teachable parts). This latter form of knowledge about pedagogy highlights and, to some degree, dispels a common distinction advocated by (particularly primary/elementary) teachers between those who teach students and those who teach subjects.[2] Also illustrated in this dual understanding of pedagogy is that knowledge of good teaching is not internally settled and is often complex. Neither are the various explanations of good teaching well articulated with broader concerns, although accounts of 'productive pedagogies' (Lingard *et al.* 2000) have addressed this within what could be termed a sociology of pedagogy. It is work that builds on Newmann and Associates' (1996) conception of 'authentic pedagogy' – classroom practices that promote learning and achievements for all students, particularly those from disadvantaged backgrounds – and considers which pedagogies might make a difference for different groups of students.

Would-be professionals undergo long periods of advanced education and training in order to acquire this formal knowledge in exchange for society's trust, which some see as legitimating their license to exercise their self-regulated authority. Teachers usually acquire this official knowledge of the profession in universities where they are also socialized into its ranks by teacher-educators (many of whom were once school teachers themselves) and by teachers in schools (who act as their supervisors during fieldwork) (see Gale and Jackson 1997). For teacher-educators, the learning process often continues beyond an initial period of undergraduate study and on-the-job development to include doctoral studies, again engaged within contexts dominated by the teaching profession.[3] During the 1990s, efforts were made to locate aspects of teacher preparation programmes within schools rather than leave them housed in universities. This has occurred as faculties of education have come under fire for ill-equipping future teachers with the necessary abilities to manage diverse classrooms and otherwise function effectively in the school and appreciate it as an institution with its own norms and cultures. In response, university-based teacher preparation programmes have begun to look to schools and teachers' associations for the standards to which they should teach, the approaches to discipline that they should adopt, and so on.

The rationale for such a prolonged process of knowledge acquisition in teacher education is embedded in the notion that professionals must learn to confront the unexpected and to address complex problems that cannot be resolved simply through the mastery of predetermined responses. This was evident in our research among some teachers who believed that 'people who have studied in a certain field and have attained a certain level, and are continuously learning, are professionals' (T2). The importance of this kind of knowledge – of how to deal with the unexpected – to the professional's claim is not lost on teachers and student-teachers. Indeed, it is through such claims that many teachers derive their confidence as professionals. As one student-teacher explained, 'you've got to be confident in your approach' (ST2). That is, the professional persona requires learning how to project an air of certainty in the face of uncertainty: 'if you're confident and you've got your own strengths in your chosen field, I think you're a professional' (ST3).

Similarly, teachers and teacher-educators are often quick to point out that teaching is not simply a matter of imparting knowledge. As professionals, they are also required to make judgements about a range of issues related to students' development. As one teacher put it: 'students are not just there as little vessels waiting to be filled with all this knowledge. You've got to have regard for the people you're teaching' (T3). Referred to in the latter part of this comment are not just the 'how to's' of teaching but also recognition of and regard for students' particularities. Some may understand this as socio-cultural amelioration for, or as an alternative approach to, a banking concept of education that 'extends only as far as receiving, filing and storing the deposits' (Freire 1972: 46). However, traditional accounts of difference have tended to focus on what is intrinsic to individual students; frequently, their intellectual, behavioural and cultural 'deficits' (see Gale and Densmore 2000: 108–25). In this context, teachers often refer to their knowledge base as including understandings drawn from a range of professions and disciplines (among which, psychology continues to dominate), which add to their own claims to be professional.

Teacher judgements about student development are, of course, judgements *as they see them* (Furlong *et al.* 2000: 5). For example, if teachers do not believe that all students are capable of meeting the demands of cognitively complex activities, they might be less likely to value and stimulate varied abilities and intelligences of all of their students. Similarly, if teachers cannot view urban schools from the perspective of historically subjugated groups, their judgements may be inappropriate, even disrespectful, of students and their families.[4] In a similar vein, if teachers have not been educated in issues of second-language acquisition and development or if their schools do not place a programmatic emphasis on these issues, the quality of teachers' judgements and their abilities to exercise them will suffer (Dentler and Hafner 1997). Finally, if teachers do not learn to connect knowledge, science and technology to the lives, histories, cultures and everyday experiences of their students, especially those from backgrounds of poverty, or, to put it another way, if the experiences of students do not become part of the knowledge base of teachers, teacher judgements and practice will most likely, if tacitly, reflect a Eurocentric world view and reify the status quo (see Kincheloe and Steinberg 1997).

Again, in our research we found evidence that teachers' professionalism and judgements relied on explanations focused on individuals and perhaps their immediate circumstances, almost to the exclusion of broader frames of reference. For example, teachers often commented, 'I think we are professional in terms of trying to cope with behavioural problems and trying to be psychologists or trying to implement psychological strategies to help students, as well as teach them, as well as do everything else' (T1).

Interestingly, it is this jack-of-all-trades tag that can work against claims to professional status that teachers and teacher-educators make, often repositioning them in relation to expert knowledge as masters-of-none. In short, their knowledge can be seen as general rather than specialized, as partial rather than fully informed and as dated rather than current. It is not just teachers who are compared in this way with specialists in particular substantive areas, but also teacher-educators. One common critique is that teacher-educators are too removed from the 'real' world of teaching in schools, that they lack 'professional currency', as some put it. As noted above, in some cases the resonance of this critique has resulted in shifting the location of teacher preparation from universities to schools, providing 'on-site' classes for practising, yet uncredentialed, teachers. Another common critique of teacher-educators is that they lack discipline depth. In this vein, one of the most recent reviews of teacher education in Australia (Ramsey 2000) suggested, at least in part, that the knowledge required by teachers cannot always be provided by faculties of teacher education. Some have noted other shortcomings in some teacher-educators' understandings. At one institution, for example:

> Cohorts of teachers-in-training and graduate teachers arrive at the University from overseas throughout the year to undertake short-term professional development programs. There are some teacher-educators in the faculty who are literate in the visitors' cultural understandings and are able to draw on both western and 'oriental' ideas in ways that are both relevant and sensitive to these students' needs. However, other faculty members appear to have neither the skills nor the resources to engage with these exchanges in ways that would reciprocally expand or internationalize the knowledges of either the teachers-in-training or themselves.
>
> (Danaher *et al.* 2000: 59)

More generally, some suspect that the professional claim to expert knowledge is greater than the knowledge professionals actually possess; that their 'bark' is better than their 'bite'. We know that no one has complete knowledge; that new knowledge can and is being created and, in some circumstances, challenging what we previously (thought we) knew. Take, for example, Christopher Columbus' exploration of the Americas, which challenged the notion of a flat world, and, even more recently, the reassessment (aided by the Hubble telescope) of the age of the universe, downsized from 16 billion years to between 8 to 12 billion years! Similarly, critical multiculturalists or anti-racists have shed light on how the knowledge we consider official and neutral is only so if we dismiss the cultural and power-related dimensions of knowledge production. In short, critics of the professional persona are not convinced that professionals are justified in making autonomous judgements on the basis that they possess more or expert knowledge. Rather, they argue for more democratic and participatory forms of decision making and for public involvement in determinations of what is and is not ethical practice, which are better understood as social and political decisions. These are matters we take up more vigorously below.

We know *best*

Notwithstanding this analysis, professionals regularly claim that they should be allowed to make decisions in particular situations that relate to their areas of expertise, free from (outside) interference. One reason offered for this desire for autonomy is that not only do professionals (presumably) know best, given their expert knowledge, but they are also able to critique and, thereby, rework their own knowledge in response to changing circumstances. Again, the argument is that the professional is one who is 'continuously learning' (T2). Despite her negative self-assessment, the following teacher's comments exemplify this notion of the reflexive professional, engaging with the apparent shortcomings in her practice. To some extent, this reflexivity, frequently championed by teachers and teacher-educators, provides one way to redress the currency and, therefore, legitimacy of teacher knowledge. It also harbors a sense of the 'confessional' (Shacklock and Smyth 1998): 'I don't think I'm a professional because I know there are so many things I can't do and I could change. I say, "I should have done that better" or "I should have been a little bit more professional"' (T4).

While there is evidence here of the professional questioning one's own expertise, in practice it tends to have validity only when it comes from within the profession and usually when it is engaged by individuals concerning themselves; a private and isolated self-examination. Indeed, autonomy presumes the right to make judgements regardless of and/or apart from the viewpoints of others. This danger has been successfully highlighted by New Right critics who have persuaded many that claims for autonomy function primarily to protect teachers from public accountability (see Chapter 2). Importantly, reflexivity signals a particular relationship between knowledge and action. Specifically, professionals are imagined to possess expertise in performing set tasks and are involved in judgements about the broad purposes to which those tasks are put. Curiously, while teachers often self-identify as professionals, the degree to which they are typically involved in making determinations about the broad purposes to which their work is put is questionable. Self-contained classrooms and new forms of school management that, in some cases, give teachers significant say in school affairs, suggest substantial autonomy and control over their work and workplace, while university degrees imply pedagogical and discipline expertise. Yet teachers' 'professional' functions are often technical (White 1983) or practical in nature. In many schools and even some faculties of education, the habitual way of doing things patterns teachers' practices to a greater extent than does theoretical, specialized knowledge.

Professional autonomy is frequently claimed on the basis that professionals often encounter situations requiring judgements to be made on the spot and not by others removed from practice, as the student-teacher (ST1) above suggests. Individual autonomy on the job also affords professionals the discretion they believe they need to act in the best interests of their clients. To guard against individuals who might use this autonomy to advance their own self-interests (particularly at the expense of others), professionals regulate their behaviour through a standard or code of ethical practice, collectively determined and monitored. The presumption here is that professionals are first and foremost concerned for the welfare of their clients – those on whose behalf they make judgements – and are motivated by a broad sense of public service. On the basis of these motivations and their expert knowledge, professionals are afforded autonomy in their practices and their work environments, albeit within the broad requirements of the law. Rather than being directed by the state in how to pursue citizens' interests, it is their code of ethics that provides the primary reference point for their actions. In short, professionals judge for themselves what constitutes good practice as well as incompetence, and otherwise set standards for their work. Moreover, those who fail to keep and/or disregard these standards are regarded as not engaged in professional behaviour, a determination that at times can appear somewhat paradoxical:

> A professional educator is someone who doesn't need a code of ethics to practice. That's because my definition of a profession is an area that is above a code of ethics . . . they're above suspicion, by implication. I'm not saying that there's not a code of ethics but a code of ethics isn't what drives what professionals do.
>
> (TE1)

These moral aspects of professional work are nevertheless uppermost in teachers' minds. It is only exemplary behaviour that qualifies as professional practice and teachers are very aware that their actions are held up to public scrutiny. Again, it is a role that many aspiring teachers regard as part of their professional persona: 'You've got to be really positive and a highly respected role model' (ST4); 'A professional is somebody who sets an example for others to follow' (ST5).

Yet, it is at the level of public acknowledgement that many teachers and teacher-educators in western cultures have failed to grasp all the privileges of professionalism. Historically, while doctors and lawyers have been granted high status, the status of teachers has been more problematic. Given: (1)

their time spent studying in their area of expertise; (2) that their practice is believed to be essential for the good of society; and (3) their position in the division of labour and the social power this carries, most professionals have demanded and won special privileges. Hence, relative to other workers in most western societies, professionals have high incomes, social prestige, access to resources, authority over the work of others and freedom from immediate supervision.

Again, we see a discrepancy between teachers' work situations and their views of themselves as professionals. This discrepancy has led some scholars to examine teacher professionalism as an ideology rather than as an object-ive description of their work. As an ideology, teacher professionalism has been manipulated and transformed by different interests and for different purposes, in a complex and contradictory process and in different historical periods (Johnson 1972; Larson 1977; Grace 1978; Ozga and Lawn 1981; Lawn and Ozga 1988; Burbules and Densmore 1991). Thus, professionalism has served as a symbol intended to legitimate differences between occupa-tional groups (Larson 1977; Hoyle 1982), differences not only in the work that is done but also the status attributed to such work.

Then there are the hierarchies amongst the professions. Howsam *et al.* (1976), for example, distinguish between what they see as 'classic' (for example, law, medicine, theology, academia), 'new' (for example, architec-ture, engineering, optometry, accounting) and 'emergent' (for example, teaching, nursing, policing) professions; the latter's professional status gains legitimacy through social acceptance and the relocation of their preparation to universities as much as through conforming to particular professional practices. On this issue, Eric Hoyle (1982) characterizes the status claims of particular occupations as 'professionalization' and the focus on the quality of practice as 'professionalism'. As implied above, the professionalization of teaching in the post-Second World War period has been evident particularly through the efforts of teacher unions (Henry *et al.* 1988) as much as teach-ing has approached particular standards of professionalism.

Similarly, Johnson (1972) explains differences between the professions in terms of the amount of control each exercise over the professional-client relationship. 'Collegiate' professions, for example, define both their clients' needs and how these should be met (doctors and lawyers being the classic examples), whereas professional 'patronage' (that of accountants, for ex-ample) involves determining the manner in which client needs are to be addressed, in situations where these needs are client defined. In Johnson's (1972) schema, teaching is best described as a 'mediated' profession. In this model, a third party (such as the state) determines for both parties in the professional-client relationship the needs of clients and how these should be addressed. However teacher professionalism is positioned in relation to other professions, for our purposes the primary question remains: does profes-sionalism, as traditionally viewed, further educators' attempts to effectively address the needs of diverse students, including preparing them to both function in and enhance the quality of democracy in society? We believe not, especially given its connotations of superior status and claims to neutrality in the face of educational inequalities and social injustices. Indeed, Johnson's (1972) work, which draws attention to who controls aspects of professional–client relations, are issues central to these concerns and which we take up more fully below.

We *deserve* recognition

If it is not already apparent, it is important to recognize that 'profession' and 'professional' are terms that invoke the principle of 'merit'. This is the belief that jobs and job-related rewards should go to those individuals who have the greatest aptitude and skill for specific tasks and that their abilities deserve recognition in the form of special entitlements (Gale and Densmore 2000: 14–17). Indeed, the relationships between task, ability and entitlement are so strong in the discourse of merit that those located in prestigious positions and occupations are frequently attributed with higher levels of ability and, therefore, deserving of greater rewards. There is also an implicit belief that outstanding abilities are distributed throughout populations only in small numbers. Thus, many people take for granted a hierarchical division of labour where there are relatively few high-status, high-paying jobs requiring sophisticated conceptual work, whereas there are many more jobs that pay less and presumably require less skill and less knowledge. Disparities of income, working conditions, salaries and social status are considered legitimate because the positions at the top of the hierarchy are, we are told, awarded upon an objective measure of one's education, training and competence.

However, Young (1990) argues that evaluating an individual's expertise above that of others inevitably involves using value-laden and culturally specific criteria and, therefore, questions the purported basis of the existing division of labour. For Young, the principal problem with the existing division of labour is that it is hierarchically structured in terms of jobs that allow for and encourage individuals to develop and exercise their conceptual and creative capacities and those that minimize these opportunities. The former, few in number, come with the highest salaries and the most social power, whereas the majority of jobs offer lower salaries and are generally less valued by social conventions. One feature of these differences is the variation in levels of control that workers have over their work. For example, professionals are typically expected to create and design their own work whereas para- and nonprofessionals are expected to execute plans made by those with more expertise. Yet many teachers and teacher-educators are increasingly expected to carry out the mandates and designs of 'higher' authorities rather than exercise their professional discretion. As one teacher described these contemporary working conditions, 'you have to take into account the school – the school's attitude and policy – and you have to act in accordance with that' (T4). While at one level we agree with the sentiments in this remark, the predominance of this view in contemporary educational contexts necessarily frames what it means to be a professional. For example: 'in the context of the school, being a professional teacher means you've got a duty to perform and that is to educate children' (T3). A third teacher makes this point more clearly: 'My experience of teachers is that they maintain their professionalism in terms of the strategies of the school: following the correct procedures that the school has outlined, doing the right thing by the Board [of Education] and doing the right things by the students themselves' (T5).

In this sense, educating students and generally 'doing the right thing' by them means executing professional judgements (about curricula, pedagogy, assessment, and so on) that are made somewhere else. The following comment, recently made by the reading specialist within an informal gathering of teachers in a primary/elementary school staff room, illustrates clearly this surrender of professional judgement by teachers: 'I'm so excited. I just visited every first grade classroom and each teacher was on the same problem of the same page at the same time. We're finally getting it down!' (T6). 'It' referred to a recently purchased district-wide skills-based reading programme, proclaimed to be especially effective with low-income English language learners.

In some cases, this particular division of labour is efficient and even desired by professionals, paraprofessionals and nonprofessionals alike. And standardized curricula (and testing) is one way through which underserved communities feel more confident that their children are receiving the same educational lessons as more privileged youth (Nieto 2000). However, along with Young (1990), the point we wish to make is not that specialization is wrong or that all hierarchies of authority in the workplace are unjust, nor even that all employees should receive identical salaries. Rather, our concern is that teachers and teacher-educators (like students and other employees) should and could have work that allows them to continually develop and exercise their skills, judgement and creative potential. When priorities, regulations and standards are established at a distance that does not allow for local modification, professional development suffers. As teachers and teacher-educators improve upon their abilities to make sophisticated pedagogical decisions, they become valuable contributors to decision-making processes within classrooms, schools and universities.

Indeed, 'recognitive' conceptions of social justice (Gale and Densmore 2000: 17–26) require that employees have at least shared decision-making power over matters that affect them in their work, repudiating the notion that only some categories of employees properly have authority in the workplace or the right to enjoy work that is both secure and rewarding financially and intellectually. Similarly, good teaching depends upon teachers and teacher-educators being sensitive to: (1) students' responses to different lessons; (2) their relationships with students; (3) the multiple interactions that affect their work in the classroom; and (4) knowing when and how to change course. Conceived in this way, the nature of teaching is highly complex, involving considerable expertise and requiring teachers and teacher-educators to constantly learn and adapt. Below we explore how this expertise might inform a reinvigorated and transformative role for teachers and teacher-educators. First, however, we consider some contemporary trends in schooling and teacher education and how these are affecting teacher professionalism.

We deserve *recognition*

Since the nineteenth century, schooling and teacher education have been regulated and, in the main, provided by the state. Recognizing this, and that teachers and teacher-educators are state employees, helps us to understand the sources and nature of new controls over and within schools as well as the possible outcomes of various strategies of educational reform (Dale 1989). Clearly, not everything that goes on in schools and faculties of education is controlled by or even related to the state. Still, a brief analysis of the capitalist state, as the primary provider of education, can help us identify significant problems facing educational systems in capitalist countries, new practices of social control, the current social division of labour and its effects on the very functioning of schooling and teacher education.

Drawing on Offe (1984, 1985), Dale (1989) contends that contemporary educational restructuring is largely the state's response to its need to guarantee the continued expansion of capital and to legitimate the capitalist system. Whitty *et al.* (1998) explain that there are at least two ways in which the state attempts to gain such legitimacy. First, it conceals what or who is responsible for the inherent inequities of capitalism. Secondly, it seeks to legitimate its own activities by disguising its relationship with capital through its posture of benign neutrality. By 'explaining economic decline and enduring poverty in terms of failures within the state infrastructure, attention is deflected away from the essential injustices and contradictions of capitalism. The management of the public sector is called into question and the demands for reform prevail' (Whitty *et al.* 1998: 44).

We suspect we are witnessing the kinds of reforms to schooling and teacher education proposed today because of the state's need to deflect attention away from problems such as increasing economic and social polarization. While in the past, attempts to justify the state as a benign mediator between the demands of poverty and wealth, and as a counterweight to economic instability (the Keynesian model), could only rely on increasing bureaucracies and interventions by 'neutral experts', today these 'solutions' are seen as the problem (Whitty *et al.* 1998). Hence, contemporary efforts to restructure schooling and teacher education frequently involve trying to make educational sites function less like a government bureaucracy and more like business. The consequences of this stance are that while teachers' and teacher-educators' work has both similarities *and* differences with work in the private sector and other state sectors, popular opinion is being manipulated to advance the notion that government-established schools and universities should be run like businesses (Walker and Barton 1989). Underpinning these efforts is the belief that the best economic system is one that is market-based, where market forces are allowed unimpeded action and influence. In this account, schools and faculties of teacher education should be subject to the rule of market competition.

While the extent to which market mechanisms can be installed in schools and universities remains an open question, as is the extent to which corporate management practices and goals will be successful, it is instructive to recognize this tendency and to examine it for its potential impact on teachers, teacher-educators, students and members of their surrounding communities. That is, called into question is the premise that a market approach necessarily delivers the best outcomes for those most intimately involved in the education process and even for others who, for all intents and purposes, stand to gain from a marketized form of education. At the same time, we must not forget that education *already* operates within a market because of its role in reproducing capitalist social relations and value systems and, therefore, that inequalities *already* exist (Power 1992: 498). Hence, contemporary proposals for increased responsibility and autonomy for schools and universities and calls for greater student and parent involvement, all suggest a *new* marketization of education (see Chapter 2). Presumably, these are reforms designed to deliver greater responsiveness to consumers and increased academic effectiveness, contributing both economic prosperity and increased quality of life for all. However, Ball (1994a) argues that the market label only *appears* to grant autonomy to schools (and universities) and only *appears* to give greater power to students and parents. In reality, the state retains considerable control over education goals and processes (see Chapter 3) – controls referred to in the higher education context as 'steering at a distance' (Kickert 1991; Marceau 1993) – which continue to systematically disempower working-class students and their parents.

As noted in Chapter 2, after studying school 'choice' in five countries, Whitty *et al.* (1998) found that market reforms do not provide equal choice for all parents of schoolchildren. Given their financial and political power, affluent parents exercise priority in the choice of schools for their children, which is not available to many working-class and middle-class parents. In a context where governments are cutting back on social services and privatizing once public institutions, school 'choice', (opportunity for) increased parent participation, and new school-based management programmes tend to structurally perpetuate social inequalities rather than equalize opportunities for all students to develop their talents and for all teachers and parents to have a voice in educational decision making. Choice is also an absent presence in the university sector. While institutions of higher education are required to report with great precision on their offerings and performances, frequently on the pretext of full disclosure to the public and to inform prospective consumers of their academic 'goods', recent studies have suggested that this 'audit culture' (Strathern 2000) plays little part in influencing the institutional choices that students actually make.

Scholars have also noted that coexisting with market-based reforms is the trend toward using corporate management principles and techniques to redefine and more tightly control the nature and methods of teaching at the local level (Ball 1988; Walker and Barton 1989; Hatcher 1994; Whitty *et al.* 1998). For example, Hatcher (1996) argues that in Australia in the 1990s, private sector models of management were applied to the public sector rather than its wholesale privatization. Similarly, corporate managerialism redefined equity in terms of economic efficiency and effectiveness rather than in terms of the 'public good'. Citing Blackmore (1990), Hatcher (1996) argues that in education this tendency combined decentralization in the promotion of school-based management with increased state control via a national curriculum and new forms of teacher accountability. Similar arguments have been mounted with respect to Australian higher education. For example, Henry (1992) identifies the 'sticks' and 'carrots' of corporate managerialism utilized in the 1990s by the Australian government to refashion the university sector in more efficient and effective ways, in order to create a Unified National System. In this context, equity issues remained on the agenda only to the extent that they served and/or could be justified in terms of efficiency and effectiveness (Gale and McNamee 1994, 1995).

Increased controls on teaching through greater state intervention were evident in what Dale (1989) described as a shift from 'licensed autonomy' of the education system to its 'regulated autonomy'. This shift means that processes and practices previously left to teachers' and teacher-educators' professional judgement, or simply based on tradition, are now more closely prescribed by state departments of education and more thoroughly monitored. Foucault (1977) refers to such practices as 'hierarchical observation'; a form of surveillance that now extends beyond monitoring institutions to the level of individuals, 'confining bodies in rooms' (that is, effectively isolating colleagues from one another) and introducing a divisive 'competitive imagination' (Gale 2000) into the teaching profession. For example, in the United Kingdom, Australia and the United States, teachers' control over what and how they teach is gradually being displaced by requirements of the state (Walker and Barton 1989). Thus, in addition to overseeing the development of curricula, we find greater, more direct and detailed state imposition of procedures for determining how teachers should teach, including priorities they should set and even how many minutes to spend on the teaching of things like reading, mathematics and even 'wait time', that is, the time teachers should wait for answers from students in response to their questioning!

In short, a substantial body of critical scholarship argues that key elements of teachers' and teacher-educators' experiences include *intensification* of the work process through increased workloads and *regulation* of the work process through closer supervision and tighter structuring (Apple 1986; Lawn and Ozga 1988; Dale 1989; Hatcher 1994; Gale 2000). It is little wonder that teachers observe:

Unfortunately, in teaching there are so many other professional things that you have to do, like all the paper work. Outside of your own classroom marking and classroom preparation, there is all this other agenda that impinges on your time. But I know that comes as part and parcel of the profession . . . [although] I think that's taking away from the teaching profession itself.

(T3)

This description does not match up very well with the traditional idea of professional work. Increasingly, teaching is defined as administering particular procedures to students. These procedures, presented in the form of textbooks, curricula guidelines, standards and frameworks and standardized tests, seem to imply that a professional approach to preparing for teaching and executing lesson plans is reasonably a technical approach, discounting the social, cultural and political contexts of schooling and teacher education. Thus, solutions to low student achievement levels are to provide more detailed prescriptions for how to teach and to monitor teachers' implementation more carefully. Important spaces for teachers' professional judgement are pre-empted by prespecified, highly routinized curricula and accompanied by new teacher accountability schemes. Also noteworthy is the extent to which this reflects a gendered pattern based on degrees of work standardization.

In order to implement these controls, the new management approach defines professional accountability as individual accountability to school and faculty administrations, as opposed to group accountability defined by a collective labour contract and broad-based, shared decision making that can also transcend organizations. Underlying this new approach to management are the concepts of 'corporate culture' and 'corporate professionalism' (Danaher *et al.* 2000). In such circumstances, the loyalty and values that employees share among themselves in a workplace (for example, solidarity and public service) are replaced by values and beliefs more harmonious with the interests of the organization (for example, competitive self-interest and the importance of consumer choice) (Hatcher 1994; Whitty *et al.* 1998). These corporate interests are secured both by an appeal to an old professional 'duty of care' for clients, reworked as 'customer demand', and by the introduction of 'commercial-in-confidence' prohibitions, both restricting teachers and teacher-educators from dissenting from the corporate position (Danaher *et al.* 2000). This new business-oriented professionalism masks the increased regulation of teachers' and teacher-educators' work, severely inhibiting them from creatively employing the knowledge they possess. It also aims at shifting focus away from classroom practice and towards such activities as attending more committee meetings, processing more records and sometimes accepting performance-related pay. In effect, an attempt is being made to resocialize teachers and teacher-educators and to transform the character of their professionalism (Mac An Ghaill 1992).

We need to think *differently*

Despite these changes, the dominant view in the wider community of schools and teacher education in predominantly English-speaking, capitalist countries (and other countries with comparable economic and political systems) is that, as state functionaries, teachers maintain a stance of neutrality in relation to social issues. That is, a big part of what it means to be a professional is to make objective and impartial decisions. Subjected to such treatment, the knowledge students are taught is ostensibly free from bias and, hence, schools' and universities' operating procedures are regarded as fair. When you consider that most teachers and teacher-educators come from the dominant culture – English-speaking, white and middle class – you can understand why, historically, it has been relatively easy for them to ignore social problems and accept existing conventions. However, as Corson (1998) reminds us, the professional claim of neutrality and the corresponding approach to teaching (programmes of teacher education included) has reinforced undemocratic conditions where the interests of non-dominant groups have remained unaddressed. Importantly, then, what are typically viewed as neutral modes of operating for schools and universities as (bureaucratic) organizations, inculcated by the ideology of professionalism that places teachers and teacher-educators above and apart from the people they serve, cannot be considered democratic.

Progressive educators frequently espouse commitments to grassroots social change and to democratic workplaces. They maintain, for instance, that the struggle for public and democratic education is fundamentally linked to larger social and political struggles. Even conventional educational goals imply not only a significantly altered educational system but also the creation of a fundamentally different society. For example, the Clinton/congressional programme for the 1990s in the United States aimed to ensure that all children start school ready to learn and to increase high school graduation rates. However, achieving these goals would have required massive amounts of federal funding not only for education but also for health care and general support for the disadvantaged. In other words, we view the current situation in western capitalist countries as requiring both global and local perspectives in terms of the way in which capitalist social relations are produced and reproduced. From this perspective, the deeper roots of exploitation and inequalities and a broader range of responses become clearer. Critically, we must be able to conceive of a new kind of society within a new kind of international order, one that is not premised upon the exploitation of working people but has a more just and appropriate distribution of social wealth, therefore, mitigating uneven development, poverty, cynicism, ignorance, environmental degradation, racism and sexism.

What does this mean for teacher professionalism? The professional is traditionally exhorted to remain detached from, in contrast to committed to, social ideas and values, on the assumption that this detachment permits objectivity. Professional ideology and the training they receive in teacher education programmes can hold educators back from identifying with particular groups of students and parents, namely those who are unlike themselves: typically, low-income students of colour for whom (standard) English is a second language. Further, some educators tend to be uncomfortable with the language of power, often underestimating the power of schools and universities to make decisions about young peoples' lives, attainment levels, acceptance into higher education, and job prospects (Gale 1999a). In many urban areas throughout the United States, the United Kingdom and Australia, official admonishments for schools to improve upon 'shocking' rates of student academic failure explicitly direct administrators and teachers to ignore students' backgrounds and personal histories because all students can learn (Gale 2001a). On the one hand, this is true and, as more and more teachers know it to be true, the more reason we have to be optimistic about students' academic progress. At the same time, the implications of the fact that students come to school and university with different resources and techniques required of them for academic achievement, have been well documented by scholars (see, for example, Gale 2002).

However, when asked about the role that poverty and racism played in students' academic performance, one principal of an urban high school recently remarked: 'That's old sociology . . . that's [i.e. poverty and racism] going to be there, but the teacher's position is not to patronize the youngster . . . No, their job is to teach them' (T7). Certainly, the notion that 'all students can succeed' is inspiring, but it is not helpful when it ignores the importance of non-school related influences on school success (Gale 2001a). At the time, this principal was under tremendous pressure to increase his school's tests scores. Otherwise, his job was at risk, his school may have been 'restructured' and as for the students:

> Well, if I can't provide the leadership necessary . . . there won't be any rewards for these kids, because even though they're part of Silicon Valley where all the money is made, they don't get to participate . . . they're outside of the picture . . . students will continue getting menial jobs . . . they will stay idle and will continue to live in garages. You know we talk about being able to provide clean cities, cities without crime, safe places for people to live and when you have people who don't have these kinds of things that are going to allow them to live a decent life, people are going to get alarmed . . . You end up with negative attitudes, feeling like nobody cares. And when you don't care, and you're cornered, you're going to bite . . . If folks can't provide a decent home for their families, then they'll do other things.
>
> (T7)

While the principal is correct that schools can only do so much and that they have a specific job, reform efforts aimed at schools isolated from their communities are likely to exacerbate existing educational problems, particularly those that are market-based (Whitty *et al.* 1998; Lauder *et al.* 1999; Thrupp 1999). Instead, teachers need avenues through which to apply their expertise, strengthening their performance both in the classroom and in their students' lives more generally (see Chapter 4).

We need to think differently

One of the problems we face is that it is difficult, if not nearly impossible, to disassociate professionalism from notions of superior status and privilege. The belief in the hierarchy of academically guaranteed competences underlies multiple social divisions. Yet, because of the great potential inherent in working with and learning from students and their communities – for creative instruction and for advancing students' and communities' collective interests – it is important for educators to recognize that traditional notions of professionalism do not serve them well. More to the point, with its ambiguous usage and its emphasis on authority based on specialized expertise – a technical rationality not amenable to public debate or discussion – professionalism can both hinder and undermine efforts to achieve a greater pooling of practical and theoretical knowledge, which could be used to construct more democratic schools and societies.

In schools and universities serving diverse communities, teachers and teacher-educators could recognize the distance that tends to exist between themselves, their students and families and from their surrounding communities. They could also recognize the limitations of their knowledge and skills by allowing themselves to learn from students, parents and other community members. In contrast to the professional claim of neutrality, which implies that expert knowledge is not based on values and is therefore superior to the knowledge of non-professionals, teachers and teacher-educators could recognize that their required expertise includes knowledge that is best understood by people who are from the communities within which they are teaching. They could require themselves to understand the worldviews and interests of various groups in order to ensure that their work actually benefits their students. In such situations, parent participation and community involvement would be vital because, at times, teachers would be 'out of their depth' (Corson 1998: 16). Broad participation and involvement not only could but should challenge schooling and teacher education as we know it, releasing the creativity of communities, parents, students, teachers and teacher-educators and countering pressures to conform simply and singularly to Anglo middle-class values.

A case in point: shortly after the overthrow of apartheid, one of us visited schools and universities in the new South Africa. In one university, the faculty explained that since black South Africans were now among their student body, they, as faculty, were painfully aware of how little they knew about these students. That is, faculty members were unable to connect what they were teaching to the background experiences of their students. Understanding that in order to further the personal and intellectual development of their students they had to understand the actual conditions of their students' lives, the faculty implemented a community service requirement for themselves. Unlike many community service programmes throughout the world where *students* are required to serve marginalized peoples from depressed areas, in this South African university a majority of *faculty* voted to require such service for themselves. Most often, this took the form of providing needed services for the communities of their black South African students. In this way, knowledge from students' communities could inform teachers' pedagogy. Thus, learning from and respecting the different social groups to which their students belonged enhanced the teacher-educators' 'expert' knowledge.

Another example is of the urban environment programme, 'My Place, Our Place', introduced at Laverton Park Primary School (Melbourne, Australia) in the mid-1990s, in an area of concentrated disadvantage (Malone 1999a; Malone and Walker 1999):

> The program aimed to rehabilitate degraded natural ecosystems in the neighbourhood, equip students and the Laverton community with skills that would enable them to positively influence decision making at the local and regional level, provide the community with much needed recreational facilities, and instil a sense of pride of their 'place'.
>
> (Malone 1999a: 164–5)

What made this something other than a 'good idea' initiated by the school was that it 'was as much about getting the community into the school as getting the school into the community' (Malone and Walker 1999: 195). Hence, the central character was not simply 'Carol . . . a primary school teacher . . . [who] wrote the first grant proposals . . . [and] became the force and the voice behind the program' (p. 196). Also centrally involved was Scott, 'a local resident who lived across the road from the school' (p. 203), an unemployed parent and also the newly appointed president of the school council. Scott 'had always had an interest in education, the environment, and environmental activism' (p. 204) and provided the programme with expertise in relation to the local environment and what could be done about it. Then, when the government announced the closure of the school and hence the programme, 'he became very politically active and led the community and media campaign against the state government' (p. 204). In many ways, 'Carol and Scott are not just involved in the program: they are the program' (p. 212). They presented themselves as metaphors of the relationship and its potential between the school and the community. Scott's comments are telling in this regard, describing the programme as 'more than just an issue of planting trees or bringing back native grasses or cleaning the creek' (p. 204). For Scott, it was also about 'getting people out of their homes [and classrooms], getting together, and getting them to socialize and get some value back into their lives. In the end, the project was about people, a dedication to the work of the people' (p. 204).

Rather than viewing parents and students as novices to be tutored, these educators created opportunities to interact with people different from themselves. Such interaction can enable educators to better understand the origins of the gulf between schools and universities and their surrounding communities and so develop more culturally responsive strategies and tactics for quality teaching and learning, and leading (see Chapter 4). Moreover, in addition to improving their pedagogy, greater knowledge of students' lives outside of school and university, combined with what they know about teaching and learning, better equips teachers and teacher-educators to address a wide range of issues affecting students, such as job opportunities, health care, violence and so on. This knowledge, enriched by working relationships with community representatives, prepares teachers and teacher-educators to play a more active role in establishing and maintaining a democratic society as well as to practice a critical and culturally responsive pedagogy.

For example, rather than identifying one's community in terms of the formal education system, educators could insist that educational decision making be more inclusive and participatory and involve students, parents and caregivers, the broader labour movement, community organizations and advocacy groups; all those that have an interest in strong public schools and universities and in issues affecting students' life prospects. Working collaboratively with a wide range of groups helps educators to better understand structurally-based conflicts of interest and how this influences educational standards as well as the impact of poverty and students' degrees of wealth. Further, through broad-based collaboration, strategies for overcoming marginalization can be developed so that upon leaving school and/or university, for example, students can find work that is both financially secure and that utilizes their talents.

In our view, effective teaching includes sensitivity to, curiosity about and accountability to a school's and university's surrounding communities. Because these are very difficult issues, in some communities a starting place might be for educators to better know and communicate with students and their families. Parents have strong vested interests in the education of their children and yet, to date, have not generally been afforded real opportunities to participate in the educational process (Mills and Gale 2002). As Sparkes and Bloomer (1993) argue, a more open and collaborative occupational culture of teaching would go a long way towards replacing the historical indifference among teachers to the real interests of parents and students. This will require a shift in how teachers think about others *and* themselves. Both of these are expressed in the comments of the Laverton Primary School Principal, reflecting on the environmental education programme outlined above:

> It was about developing a system of values for life – that you have the right and ability to change your world, change your society, that you can influence it. A lot of people from this community don't believe they have the ability or right to do that. We're trying to set up something where the community would in every sense own it and make it,

would drive it and lead it to wherever it goes – empowering people to change society.

(Malone 1999b: 234–5)

Conclusion

There are at least three issues that emerge from these discussions for student-teachers, teachers, teacher-educators and their work. The first involves educators' *isolation from others*. In our view, education generally is suffering from an acute bout of competitive individualism. Shared values, if they are shared, are those determined elsewhere, typically by corporate managers and/or the state. Being a professional teacher in this context amounts to the effective and efficient performance of one's duties but there is little room for considering the worth of these, especially in collaboration with others. However, neither should the future for the profession be a return to what once was. That, too, was removed from the very individuals and communities education professionals claimed to serve. Student-teachers, teachers and teacher-educators need to (re)form collectives that mitigate against their isolation; spaces in which it is 'safe' to think differently, where difference is valued and individuals supported. Yet, these spaces also need to be inclusive of others in their communities. Forming alliances of this kind is not simply a political tactic but also recognition of the value that broad interactions contribute to schooling, teacher education and society more generally.

Second, isolation of this kind has contributed to *the closing down of debate*. The sticks and carrots of corporate managerialism, sometimes dressed in market terms of 'commercial-in-confidence', contribute to an arrogant purchase on knowledge and action that isolates and contains dissension. Work intensification, a limited scope for decision making, and the imperative to be a market leader – the 'manufactured' compression of time – also contribute to a lack of debate. There is less time for interaction and for questioning the value of current practices, producing a 'fast' professionalism. Student-teachers, teachers and teacher-educators need to combat such pressures by claiming and creating spaces and opportunities to speak of difference and to examine the value of their practices. These also need to be spaces in which to hear and address the concerns of others, as *they* see them. Simply replacing one form of arrogance with another is hardly democratic. Third, the isolation of education professionals from others and their lack of involvement in determinations that directly affect them have led to *a reduction in meaningful work*, where teachers' and teacher-educators' expertise is frequently dismissed and opportunities to contribute to working through social and institutional problems are appropriated by management. Again, such matters are not resolved simply by professionals taking back control, not that they ever fully had it. New forms of meaningful work need to be pursued in conjunction with opportunities for others to express their understandings and desires and participate in making decisions about their environment. In this account, teachers are best described in terms of: (1) their positioning in relation to others; (2) their regard for cultural and epistemological difference; and (3) their contributions to the development of others.

Our critique of traditional accounts of teachers' and teacher-educators' professionalism has not simply been concerned with delegitimating the voice of educators and deskilling their practices. We have also been aware that the 'golden age' of professionalism was not so golden and, in its own way, was exclusionary. Such understanding helps to explain why the New Right has been able to so easily capture the education agenda and place it within the increasingly visible hands of the market (Chapter 2). Within its grasp, traditional notions of professionalism have rendered teachers and teacher-educators susceptible to claims that they exclude consumer groups from genuine involvement in educational processes and institutions. In particular, teachers and teacher-educators are portrayed as self-interested and unresponsive to the business community (in not adequately preparing students to a certain standard for work) and to the desires of parents and citizens (in not adequately addressing issues of relevance and utility). Challenges for educators, then, arise at a number of levels and not simply in response to their repositioning. One important challenge is for educators to adopt the epistemological standpoint of students and their communities; in part, to address the representation of students and parents as suffering from 'provider capture' (Lauder 1991). Broader challenges are demonstrated in concerns for: (1) the kind of society we want and its expression in national policies; (2) how to provide for everyone's needs, particularly those of the most disadvantaged; (3) the extent to which these are met through the provision of public services; and (4) the place of education in redressing social injustices and inequalities.

Many countries around the world are currently experiencing systemic changes in education. How these changes, and teachers' and teacher-educators' responses to them, influence their forms of organization, their development and their identities, needs further examination. The challenge is to create means for educators to work with representatives from diverse sectors of society to discern where educators need autonomy and where incorporating perspectives from outside the school and university communities can enhance their work. If we are to translate the rhetoric of democracy and social justice in education and society into practice, we must boldly confront deeply seated notions and practices of professionalism that result in teachers' isolation from nonprofessionals and narrow debates and discussion.

Questions for discussion/research

- How can the organizational structure of a school facilitate teachers' commitment to establish working relationships with students' communities?
- How might a recognition of students' different communities inform a teacher's pedagogy and, thereby, benefit those communities?

- How useful is the notion of professionalism for teachers pursuing a radical democratic agenda for schooling? How might it be reconfigured to accommodate this?

Suggested readings

Hargreaves, A. and Evans, R. (eds) (1997) *Beyond Educational Reform: Bringing Teachers Back In*. Buckingham: Open University Press, Chapters 3 and 4.

Lawn, M. (1996) *Modern Times? Work, Professionalism and Citizenship in Teaching*. London: Falmer Press, Chapter 9.

Robertson, S. (1996) Markets and teacher professionalism: a political economy analysis, *Melbourne Studies in Education*, 37: 23–39.

Sachs, J. (2002) *The Activist Teaching Profession*. Buckingham: Open University Press, Chapter 5.

Whitty, G., Power, S. and Halpin, D. (1998) *Devolution and Choice in Education: The School, the State and the Market*. Buckingham: Open University Press, Chapter 5.

Community: reconnecting school and society

Introduction

In 1959, C.W. Mills argued that one of the major problems facing conceptions of the 'good' society was the false separation between public issues
and private troubles. Today such problems persist, not just in a theoretical
but also in a political and socio-economic sense. What has changed, however, is a shift in the dominant discourse of western democracies, which has
repositioned many public issues as private troubles. Schooling, for example
– along with health care, housing, unemployment and provisions for the
elderly – is increasingly perceived as a private matter for negotiation by
individual schools, teachers, students and parents. Consumer choice has
become the catch-phrase of neoliberal education policy although, as noted
in preceding chapters, many of these 'consumers' seem to have fewer real
choices. In this chapter we suggest that the seemingly private troubles of
many students, particularly those schooled within growing concentrations
of poverty and those marginalized on the basis of race and ethnicity, are
matters of significant public concern. Similarly, we question business dominance of public life and its impact on schooling. Drawing on Young (1990),
we argue that schools need to move beyond traditional public/private distinctions, to conceive of their diverse communities as spaces in which to
share their commonalties *and* differences and to take pleasure in exploring
these, while also allowing for overlap and intermingling without leading
to homogeneity. We examine what such conditions for public life might
mean for social and economic policy and for teachers and schools, and how
parents and students can be repositioned in this new accounting of school
communities.

Guiding questions/issues

In earlier chapters we noted that a general pattern of reforms that place
a variety of demands on schools, administrators, teachers, students and
the general public has been discernable in the western world since the late

1970s, although this has become more apparent in recent times. New forms of governance and financial management in educational institutions, business-inspired curricula, increased emphasis on testing, increased parental choice among schools and more overt accountability measures are some reforms reflecting larger economic, social and political realignments. The globalization of capital and the growth of financial markets are also changing our engagement with work: creating new jobs, eliminating old jobs and changing how work in general is organized. Schooling ultimately responds to these trends and pressures not only in what population goes to which school and how teachers work, but also in what is being taught.

Arguably, these connections between schooling and its larger context suggest that teachers' responsibilities extend beyond their classrooms and schools to their students' communities and to the quality of life and nature of democracy in their societies more generally. However, given many teachers' own life experiences, frequently informed by white middle-class cultures, they can often be unaware of the 'public issues' that concern low-income communities and sometimes even unaware of their 'private troubles' (Mills 1959). Even when teachers and others recognize the latter, these are not always seen as connected with the former, and vice versa. In this chapter we attempt to draw attention to these public issues and private concerns and to make connections between them. In doing so, we address the conditions found in many students' communities, including those of their public schools. In particular, we ask three critical questions about values and schooling:

- What do 'equality', 'freedom' and 'justice' mean in contemporary western societies?
- What role should schools play in relation to these values?
- Will quasi-market school reforms remove the primary obstacles to enabling all young people to live hopeful and successful lives in their communities?

In considering these questions, we suggest that the current plethora of market-based 'solutions', including their discourses and values, have limited possibilities and often divert attention away from more fundamental economic, social and political problems. Instead, we argue that a different conception of 'revitalization' is needed in school communities, one that is informed by a radical democratic agenda (Lummis 1996). Our arguments in this chapter are largely informed by our reading of contemporary academic research and scholarship, although our own research among teachers, principals and decision makers in school districts provides some collaborating data. We begin our reading of these issues with a brief account of the socio-economic conditions of our communities, particularly their segregation and stratification along social class lines and the consequences for schooling and students' academic achievement. We argue that the legitimization of these separations are informed by a shift in our socio-economic sensibilities; a shift identified in Chapter 2 as being to the New Right of politics and which we also regard as emphasizing private troubles at the expense of public issues in education.

We conclude that this false separation of public and private needs to be redressed at global as well as local levels if we are to begin to establish conditions for democratic schooling.

The socio-economic conditions of our communities

At the beginning of the twenty-first century, urban areas in predominantly English-speaking, capitalist societies are often characterized by extreme economic and social polarizations, complex ethnic and racial mixes, segregated neighbourhoods and the increasing migration of low-income peoples as intra- and inter-national refugees. Within these urban areas, wealthy neighbourhoods or enclaves resemble walled cities that are intended to provide security and peace of mind to insulate insiders from those outside their walls; white urban areas of some South African cities perhaps providing the archetype, but examples are also found throughout the world. In many large western cities, corporate towers, luxury apartments and hotels loom metaphorically as well as literally over the homeless: people of all ages wrapped in well-worn blankets, old newspapers and cardboard, who sleep in parks and doorways next to shopping carts and carry-bags holding whatever else they may possess. The distinctions between 'them' and 'us' hardly seem to have been more acute, so much so that some wonder how much wider the gulf between an emerging urban gentry and the destitute will grow.

For many advanced economies, this gap between the 'haves' and 'have-nots' was crystallized in the public consciousness in the latter half of the twentieth century. During this period, it became apparent that for many people the income of one person in a household, or the benefits one gets from work, could not cover the basic needs of that household. A number of changes in the social and economic fabric of these societies seemed to contribute to their circumstances. In the United States and the United Kingdom, for example, a massive influx of non-English-speaking peoples working in low-wage sectors put additional strains on public services, including education. At the same time, a welfare backlash in most western nations drastically reduced government funds for social services and produced increasingly selective principles of social welfare, while decades of de-industrialization invited the privatization of the public sector and called for volunteer and philanthropic remedies to persistent social problems. The economic and political orthodoxy of neoliberalism and the New Right, which informed these reforms, maintained that an expanded public service sector (post-WWII) drained resources from profitable private sector investment, whereas a free market encouraged more stringent and effective deployment of resources (see Chapter 2). Taking on this rhetoric, and/or in response to governments' retreat from public sector provision, the urban middle to upper classes increasingly paid only for those services that benefited themselves: private security guards, private road repairs, private parks, private health clubs and private schools (see, for example, Reich 1991: 42). Those who could afford to do so, continued to enjoy the benefits of these services; others who could not, increasingly relied on charity or simply went without.

An historical review of community health care is instructive in highlighting these inequalities. Discussing the link between child poverty and disease (tuberculosis and asthma, for example), Sue Brooks (2000) explains how public health issues were not always construed as a private responsibility, due to individual risk factors (ascribed to their genes, for example), personal misfortune or irresponsibility. On the contrary, early in the twentieth century the health of children in most western societies was considered a matter of public responsibility, requiring the elimination of social and political problems such as crowded housing and poor nutrition. Yet, the irony of repositioning health as a private matter is that contemporary extremes of social inequities may, once again, spread infectious, preventable diseases on a public scale. In a more nuanced account, Richard Wilkinson (1996) concludes that within developed countries, the relationship between overall public health and inequalities in levels of income is a matter of relative rather than absolute income levels. That is, regardless of a society's aggregate wealth, public health inevitably declines when there are significant differences between income levels. We suspect that the same could be said of public education.

Increasing economic stratification is complicated by the fact that many ethnic and racial divisions run along class lines, particularly in the United States but also elsewhere in countries such as in Australia and the United Kingdom. Thus, rather than representing a benign blend of social classes, we find more often that residential communities are sharply segregated and stratified (see, for example, Gillborn and Youdell 2000). This is despite the fact that many of the academic discourses around ethnicity and gender in education do not sufficiently acknowledge the existence of social class (Aronowitz 1997; Yates 2000). In our view, the ongoing processes of stratification and segregation, which result in impoverished communities at a number of levels, represent some of the most pressing problems currently facing educators. While urban ghettos typically possess 'riches' (for example, strong social ties and rich cultural traditions) not readily apparent to the casual observer, these strengths are subjected to seriously debilitating conditions such as high levels of un/underemployment, crime, job insecurity, poor health conditions and inadequate and/or unsafe housing (Kozol 1995). For example, while recent statistics indicate that unemployment is declining in the United States, this conceals that the increasing incarceration of young black males subtracts two percentage points from unemployment statistics (Freeman 1995). Children in low-income communities, often children of colour, are also subjected to acts of prejudice, discrimination and racism on a daily basis. Critically, the problem of materially debilitating conditions is not due to a lack of resources or information. Rather: 'Racial demographics have proved to be a critical determinant of environmental quality . . . Private and governmental research has identified significant disparities in the placement of waste sites, enforcement of environmental laws, remedial action, location of clean-up efforts, and the quality of clean-up strategies' (Lively 1994: 311).

These factors – race, ethnicity and class – combine to increase residential segregation: often referred to as 'white flight', although middle-class people of colour and others who have middle-class aspirations often vacate inner cities as well. At the same time, some inner city areas are being refurbished and the privileged are moving back in. In such cases many of the poor are effectively banished, unable to afford to live there any longer.

The consequences for schooling, students' academic achievements and life chances

The growing polarization of incomes, levels of child poverty, rates of gentrification and persistent racial and ethnic antagonisms in such countries as the United States, the United Kingdom and Australia have resulted in many young people being educated in segregated schools. Several commentators now believe that democratic and socially just expectations for public schooling have been betrayed – as measured by persistent differential academic achievement among gender, social class and racial/ethnic groups – given that the educational opportunities available to children are so vastly unequal despite educational expansion.[1] Because their families possess insufficient material and esteemed cultural resources, many poor children attend underfunded and understaffed schools, with low status and less political support than neighbouring districts and where poor academic performance is expected or at least anticipated (Connell 1993; Yates 2000). This is despite the fact that some ethnic groups in these circumstances have demonstrated that high academic achievement is possible given strong community and family support (Franklin 2000; Tsolidis 2000). Nevertheless, the high degree of segregation (informed by social class, race and ethnicity) between schools highlights gross social inequalities in the provision of public schooling.

Students living in working-class areas, often with large proportions of ethnic minorities, disproportionately attend schools with 'less favourable characteristics' – in relation to school size, stability of student population, staff experience and expertise – *at each stage of their schooling* (Lauder *et al.* 1999: 129). This points to the cumulative effect of schooling on students' academic performance, which is typically lower in low-income schools than in middle-class schools (Balfanz 2000; Nieto 2000; Sanders 2000). Although some schools may function relatively smoothly with students performing well on standardized tests, in many areas academic achievement gaps, especially those between students differentiated by social class, race and ethnicity, are actually widening (Gillborn and Youdell 2000; Olsen 2001). If one accepts the research on the social construction of difference – that is, on average, members of socially defined groups are more or less equally capable of academic success (Connell 1993; Brint 1998) – then the creation, reproduction and legitimation of academic inequalities among groups arises as a major concern.

While schools and neighbourhoods have often been both socially and racially segregated, contemporary choice schemes may well exacerbate this segregation by extending it into schools that were previously relatively integrated (see, for example, Gewirtz *et al.* 1995; Glatter *et al.* 1997; Whitty *et al.* 1998). Indeed, this has been one of the effects of 'charters' in some urban schools in Australia, and in many cities throughout the United States. Students, who once might have attended their local high school, must now meet the school's particular entrance standards related to its specialization or 'charter' (music, dance, information technology, and so on). Failing that, these students can be forced to travel past their local school, and perhaps two or three others, to gain entrance into a school with no such specialization; schools that might be populated by students similarly unable to gain entrance elsewhere. Some of these students have parents who are able to afford to buy them a place at a more local private school, thereby rescuing them from their consignment yet at the same time intensifying the segregation of the student population along class lines. For such parents, their choices appear constricted rather than enhanced. Both they and those who find their children in distant schools are forced to make choices they might not otherwise have made or they have had one set of choices replaced with another.

More generally, low-income students in developed economies seem to be increasingly concentrated in poorly resourced schools. Whereas middle-class parents, already in possession of both the material and cultural capital to negotiate their way successfully through their school system, appear even better positioned with contemporary choice schemes and other market-led reforms to reassert their advantages in education and the labour market (Brown 1995). Similarly, while parent involvement is widely believed to be a critical determinant of educational performance (Epstein 1984), it has been demonstrated that the level of parental involvement is related to parents' class position and to the social and cultural resources of their families and communities (Lareau 1987), particularly as these are understood and valued by schooling.

One further consequence of segregated and stratified communities seems to be that people have fewer opportunities to confront deeply ingrained perceptions and practices of social class, racial and ethnic differences. Even when schools have been established to foster a particular ethnic/racial culture or language as the preferred option by segments of some marginalized communities, separate communities and schools have a history of being unequal entities. Indeed, it is our view that segregated schools and segregated communities can, in the long run, encourage a narrow or even chauvinistic outlook. Connell (1993) writes similarly about schooling that attempts to redress disadvantage without also reworking the 'mainstream'. In such circumstances, he argues, a 'mainstream' education is itself diminished. In a similar vein, we fear that separation and polarization have the potential to breed ignorance, hostility and even violence.[2]

In the 1990s, social class origins were not only the key predictor of academic success at school but also of future position in the labour market (Mac An Ghaill 1994). Today, students from professional and managerial families continue to have far greater chances of entering professional and managerial occupations than those from clerical or working-class families. And while there continue to be people who explain differences in academic achievement (and poverty) in terms of genetic differences between races and classes (see, for example, Herrnstein and Murray 1994), the weight of evidence is against genetics on this issue. The data show the greater importance of social environment and the ways in which income, wealth and life-chances are embedded in the social structure (Brint 1998; Lauder *et al.* 1999).

Vast differences in wealth, health, education, leisure time and general well-being between certain groups of people appear to be either generally accepted or ignored in capitalist societies. For those who are less accepting of the inevitability and desirability of these differences, it is still difficult to know how to eradicate or reduce social class disparities in society in general and between schools in particular. In the contemporary political climate, those who comment on the injustice of income disparities are often labelled as idealist or old leftist radicals, in a way that is dismissive of their critique and of any alternatives they may suggest. As Dom Helder Camara once said, 'When I give food to the poor, they call me a saint. When I ask why the poor have no food, they call me a communist.' Today's 'common sense' leads many people to believe that gross income disparities are to be expected given differences in initiative, motivation and intelligence among the general population. In this account, it seems only natural that the wealthy should educate their own children in private schools, separate from everyone else. After all, those parents who cannot afford private schools have public schools that appear similar enough to allow students, if they are capable of being educated, to receive a 'good education'; albeit, narrowly defined (see Gale and Densmore 2000).

While different parental hopes, ambitions and aspirations for their children help explain, to some extent, differential academic outcomes among groups of students, such factors do not operate independently of social class. Both inside and outside of schools, working-class students typically have much less spent on their opportunities for learning than do their middle-class contemporaries (Peshkin 2001). Further, while social class alone does not determine students' or teachers' experiences in school, the social class composition of a school's student intake, together with the power relations and resources generated by a particular socio-economic status (SES) mix, significantly affect school processes and student achievement (Anyon 1981; Connell *et al.* 1982; Lareau 1989; Metz 1990; Benn 1997; Thrupp 1999). For example, Thrupp's (1999) research suggests that three mechanisms, or some combination of them, are likely to facilitate the influence of student population characteristics on school processes: (1) reference group processes, (2) instructional processes, and (3) organizational and management processes.[3]

In drawing attention to schooling's reference group processes, Thrupp raises the possibility that low-SES students' academic achievement improves by *informal* contact with higher-SES peers (1999: 33). The argument here is that middle-class cultural and material capital, including curriculum knowledge, may be shared, to an extent, with working-class students. Thrupp (1999) also argues that through interaction with middle-class peers, working-class students may come to judge their own capabilities more favourably. Pierre Bourdieu argues similarly, that 'the work of [cultural capital] acquisition is . . . an investment, above all of time' in the company of those whose cultural capital has a positive value in relation to 'the demands of the scholastic market' (Bourdieu 1997: 48). Time in the right company seems a vague and informal criterion in relation to the transmission and accumulation of cultural capital, although in Bourdieu's account, it is the most potent.[4]

This potency, however, does not diminish the importance of Thrupp's (1999) second reference to 'instructional processes'. It is well documented that low-income schools tend to have fewer resources to use for teaching, that they frequently purchase less demanding curricula, and hold lower expectations for students, which affect the pace and complexity of the curriculum and instruction (Brantlinger 1993; Balfanz 2000). Thrupp's argument is that low-SES students' academic achievement may be increased by higher-quality instruction similar to that in middle-class schools. As noted in Chapter 5, 'authentic' (Newman and Associates 1996) and 'productive pedagogies' (Lingard *et al.* 2000) are examples of research specifically focused on classroom practices that promote learning and achievements for all students, particularly those from disadvantaged backgrounds, and on determining which pedagogies might make a difference for different groups of students.

Third, Thrupp (1999) suggests that academic achievement improves when particular organizational and management processes positively affect and are affected by the instructional work of schools. Such processes include maintaining buildings and resources, raising money, recruiting quality teachers and addressing students' broader social needs. Importantly, Thrupp is not advancing a deficit approach to the cultures of low-income peoples. Neither is he unaware of potentially damaging assimilatory effects of 'school mix'. His point is that the academic effectiveness of a school reflects both the (middle) class model of schooling in capitalist societies and the cultural and material background of students from middle-class families. Overall, schools with concentrated poverty appear to have more burdens and fewer resources that outweigh the benefits of segregated schools.[5]

In short, the class bias of western democracies systematically degrades the life chances of working-class pupils. Educators could offset these disadvantages by working with others to equalize resource distribution and focusing more on the state's role and responsibilities in supporting those conditions necessary for all individuals to maximize their development and exercise their talents. In the 1960s and 1970s such a focus was evident, even if this was predominantly at a rhetorical level. Values such as democracy, equality, social responsibility, cooperation, full employment and better social services were operative in much public policy discourse and recommendations. In contrast, excellence, choice, competition, standards, accountability, efficiency and effectiveness currently monopolize public and educational discourse. Previous policy agendas, emphasizing the multiple factors and structural problems that disadvantage particular youth, encouraged more adult work roles for students and social interventions into their circumstances. Today's educational discourse is fixated on students' test scores as though these really measure a person's character and virtues. This shift is remarkable and deserves attention if we are to think our way through what can be done to enhance all students' academic achievements and life chances.

The shift to the New Right

That western societies and their political systems have shifted to the right is frequently asserted and now goes largely uncontested. That is, the shift is now acknowledged by the broader public whereas its legitimacy seems contested only in some academic arenas. As noted in Chapters 2 and 3, one important aspect of this shift is that governments and corporations have instituted a mix of *increasing influence* over and *decreasing responsibility* towards working people, the unemployed and their communities; reconfigurations often referred to as 'steering at a distance' and 'small government'. While people with high incomes, wealth, and elite social contacts are 'doing well', many others are witnessing the decline of real wages and an increase in living costs. Government funds for education, housing, health and other social services are typically being reduced or eliminated, with the onus for their provision thrust onto individuals to acquire them through the market. In the discourse that legitimates these changes, market forces (compared to public sector institutions) are alleged to be more efficient, more democratic and a superior means for enabling consumers to obtain resources otherwise unavailable to them.

Reflecting on these matters, one policy analyst interviewed in our research pointed to ways in which those responsible for teaching and administering schools in the United States have responded to these changing policies:

> In the [19]80s there was this push for greater cultural conformity. You know, I used to laugh a little bit because Ronald Reagan kept talking about . . . if kids just had more homework, suddenly they'd be more virtuous creatures and they wouldn't be as mean spirited and cantankerous . . . These sorts of moral symbols started to be reintroduced in the political scene, and then reduced down to simple symbols like homework or doing well on test scores. So rather than viewing kids as diverse and expressive individuals, who kind of make their way into the adult world in a more multi-faceted way, we started to simplify how we really understood adolescents and understood teenagers' own

lives . . . We're [now] seeing [this simplification] in a lot of policy being directed just at the school – if we fix the schools we'll somehow raise kids' achievement, independent of what's happening in their communities or in their homes . . . It's sort of like saying, if we just have better hospitals, health conditions will dramatically rise; it's a narrowing of the overall discussion . . . These school reform efforts are yielding big political pay-offs for political leaders . . . because the whole institutionalized way of viewing the problem is inside the school . . . It's a much safer political strategy. . . . [Whereas] to talk about employment and structural problems is risky politically. [Also] most middle class parents . . . see the problem as being rooted in the schools . . . There's almost the suburbanization of urban problems so that political figures have to talk in ways that echo how the voters – how suburban, middle class voters – are viewing the problem. In the [19]60s, of course, we had a counter force, which was the Civil Rights Movement and a Poverty Movement. But with that sort of constituency gone, or at least muted under the political system, it's hard to reopen these broader issues around jobs, employment and family poverty.

Like public policy, much educational research and practice ignores the 'bigger picture' – how schools operate within their given social contexts – and concentrates instead on the details of school life (Ozga 1990). Despite the fact that the results of this approach have been devastating for many children, their families and communities, school reform efforts narrowly focused on schools, regardless of their social context, yield big political pay-offs (for politicians, businesses, corporations and intra-national bodies) and lend themselves to much of the discourse of the New Right: the lure of privatization and the absence of a democratic public.

In addressing these we revisit aspects of the discussion introduced in previous chapters, to re-emphasize the bigger picture informing education markets before considering what might be done to redress their more negative influences in schools and communities. It is precisely because nothing short of democracy itself is at stake that we have assigned special importance throughout this book to the market logic at play in the New Right's reworkings of democracy. We fear that without a clear and strong understanding of the ideological and material practices shaping the spaces within which we live, we will fail to struggle for the democratic rights we currently have and for their needed expansion in our communities.

The lure of privatization

Since the late 1970s and early 1980s, educational systems have been designed in line with the blueprints of New Right ideas and ideologies. Despite its internally contradictory and heterogeneous character (Taylor *et al.* 1997), the New Right coalition has successfully created a climate of public opinion favourable to its aims. As outlined in Chapter 2, the label 'New Right' has been applied to ideas and policies advocated by a coalition with contradictory goals. One important division within the New Right is between a 'conservative' tendency that is primarily interested in restoring cultural and political authority in society and a 'neoliberal' tendency that makes the free market the best mechanism for allocating resources. Based on the premise that, fundamentally, individuals do and *should* pursue their private interests – to satisfy their personal needs for education, health, housing and so on – in general, government regulation ('interference') is frowned upon except when it protects the free market, that is, when it preserves the 'spoils' of market activity (such as the maintenance and acquisition of property and capital) as well as the freedom to engage in market activities (such as the exchange of goods and services). In this context, business monopolies are acceptable, although monopolies of the state or labour unions are not. The pursuit of social justice or equity is also problematic because it presumes the public interest should define and plan for particular social and economic outcomes, whereas in the marketplace, individual freedoms and rights are given absolute reign, except when controls are necessary to ensure favourable market conditions. Similarly, democracy is valued primarily for the freedom to compete. From this perspective, the best way to ensure these values is to strengthen the global capitalist economic market.[6]

A brief account of 'public choice theory' in particular is helpful in explaining why right-wing sentiments tend to embrace market relations and caution against radical democratic and community processes. According to such theories, 'heavy' government spending is the result of various special interest groups, such as teachers' unions, which successfully exert their influence on the state to allocate its revenue in ways that advance their particular agendas. Generous state expenditures are also blamed for the high national debt, which increased the levels of inflation in the 1970s and 1980s. In this way both state government and democratic political processes are represented as creating the economic crisis. Applied to education, democratic control of schooling, exercised through bureaucratic processes, results in interest groups such as teachers' unions securing higher teacher salaries and improved working conditions, neither of which are believed to be responsible for improved academic performance. The market solution, then, involves reform of public education through mechanisms of privatization (vouchers, for example) and by weakening the role and influence of teachers' unions.

While a number of criticisms can be directed against the assumptions embedded in public choice theory, two of these especially concern us in this chapter. The first is the assertion that we should strive toward an economic model of perfect competition and the second is that democracy is a problem because it allows vested interests to prevail. With regard to the first, because we live in a distinctively capitalist society, any market will reflect the antagonisms of the social class structure. Social classes and communities do not come to a market with equal resources and, therefore, cannot compete on 'equal' terms. Capitalist markets embody ever-expanding competitive commodity relations and, arguably, further the social disintegration and segregation discussed above. Once commodity production is dominant, goods and services of necessity are produced for profit, rather than for our use. While use value is a *sine qua non* of all production, the *purpose* of exchange under private ownership of production is profit. In such circumstances, 'there is not much space left' (Gorz 1992: 179) for the development of different kinds of cooperative social and community relations to enjoy, protect or promote the common good. Needs are artificially created and satisfied (for some) by commodity production and exchange. Even though markets are portrayed as neutral spheres of freedom and choice, they are substantively biased, preserving existing unequal relations of wealth and privilege. Contemporary capitalist markets are 'the supreme institution of winners and losers, with the winners imposing their power on the losers without redress' (Ranson and Stewart 1994: 49).[7]

Such analysis has profound implications for the education marketplace. For example, proponents of consumer 'choice' contend that all parents in time will make informed decisions about which school to send their children. As noted in Chapter 2, the proposition is that schools subsequently will be required to compete for students, driving up school performance and increasing diversity among students at any one given school. Under-performing schools will go out of business and teachers will be more motivated to improve their teaching (Whitty *et al.* 1998). There is, however, considerable inequality of parental choice based on social class, gender and ethnicity (Gewirtz *et al.* 1995). Moreover, in their study on New Zealand schools, Lauder *et al.* provide powerful evidence that markets 'are likely to lead to a decline in overall educational standards because they have a negative effect on the performance of working-class schools, while leaving middle class schools untouched . . . in effect, education markets trade off the opportunities of less privileged children to those already privileged' (Lauder *et al.* 1999: 2). Inequality of parental choice, together with the potential harmful consequences for students who remain in public schools after some parents have removed their children (Lauder *et al.* 1999; Thrupp 1999), problematize the notion that market competition can raise educational standards overall.

A second criticism of public choice theory is that it marginalizes equality, defined in terms of 'vested interests'. While there are real limits to the forms of democracy we are witnessing at the beginning of the twenty-first century, a regard for social justice demands a regard for democracy in a radical 'intensified' form (Lummis 1996). We agree with Young (1990) that the problem with interest-group decision making is not that people promote their own interests, but that all people do not have equal resources, organization or power to voice their interests, nor the self-confident social privilege to feel anyone's equal, in a museum, at a university, in a public meeting and so on. Whereas democracy formally provides valuable protections, such as the freedom of association, diversity of opinion and checks on state power, it cannot effectively challenge the exercise of power relations within a capitalist economic system (see Chapter 1). The power of private property, its imperative to maximize profits and to distribute resources for its accumulation, defines our daily lives but remains essentially untouched by democracy (Wood 1999). Democracy presupposes that social and economic equality is not a necessary condition for 'participatory parity' in public spheres (Fraser 1997: 69–98). Yet, even after formal restrictions on the rights of people of colour, women and/or workers to participate in public bodies or forums have been eliminated, this does not guarantee that their voices can make substantive decisions on public policy (see Chapter 3). Race, gender and class disadvantages often continue to operate, albeit informally. Increasingly, features of both our economy (such as corporations, production, the labour market, trade and commerce) and civil society (educational opportunity, environmental standards, health care options and so on) are removed from substantive democratic accountability.

The current tendency to identify democracy with the 'free market' (as freedom of choice, for example) and with 'privatization' seriously impedes progress not only toward further historical development of democracy but even toward its full realization. Even legal provisions that we might hope would protect democracy, including social services for immigrants to the United States, the United Kingdom and Australia, and for Mexican citizens working in *maquiladoras* in Mexico, are easily manipulated. By way of illustration, the North American Free Trade Agreement (NAFTA) provides numerous examples of serious curtailments of civil liberties under western democracies. NAFTA, signed by Canada, the United States and Mexico, which was supposed to promote democracy through free trade, now threatens the protections of the Constitution and Bill of Rights that guarantee civil rights in the United States. Specifically, a NAFTA provision (Chapter 11) invests a three-judge tribunal, appointed by corporations, with the power to abrogate the rights of citizens to their own property and to health, environmental and labour standards whenever these are ruled tantamount to expropriating the earnings of foreign investors. Already the government of Mexico has paid huge tax revenues for potential losses that a United States corporation claimed for not operating a toxic dumpsite in Mexico.

The absence of a democratic public

Historically, working-class families have placed their hopes in public education to equip their children with the skills, knowledge and dispositions necessary for social mobility and the capacity for citizenship (Brint 1998; Sanders 2000). Like many educators, they have believed that each child should be provided with equal educational opportunities. This belief in the worth of every individual and their right to develop their talents has been an ideological tenet of democracy. Public schools are correctly perceived as a key institution for promoting these values, with the potential for children from different backgrounds to sit next to and work with one another, learning about one another in the process. The hope is that this helps prevent prejudice formation and intolerance caused when different social groups are isolated from one another. The challenge for education systems today of increasing diversity presents opportunities for developing democratic dimensions of public education. Bhikhu Parekh (1986), for example, defines the possibilities for multicultural education as 'an education in freedom – freedom *from* inherited biases and narrow feelings and sentiments, as well as freedom *to* explore other cultures and perspectives and make one's own choices in full awareness of available and practicable alternatives' (p. 26, original emphasis).

Clearly, public schools have the potential to widen the horizons of children, enabling students to better form their own educated views and enabling society to benefit from the experiences and contributions of diverse social sectors. However, the marketization of education detracts from that potential. This is because a consumer-oriented approach to schooling stratifies educational experiences, assuring privileged parents that their children are 'gaining' or 'winning' over others (Whitty *et al.* 1998; Labaree 2000; Peshkin 2001). In brief, a focus on individuals pursuing their own self-interests and interacting with schools as consumers rather than as citizens sidelines the democratic purposes of education and exemplifies the dominance of economic goals (Labaree 1997). Further, while politicians encourage us to frame these issues in terms of parental rights, individual freedoms and self-determination, this shift away from the democratic purposes of schooling to a competitive, economic purpose reflects a narrow and self-defeating conception of 'private', one that denies the context needed in order for 'private' developments to thrive.

Throughout western democracies many people believe that capitalism has triumphed worldwide as the best and most desired way to organize an economic system. This worldview feeds the central claims of the New Right: that public issues of housing, education, health care, provisions for the elderly, and so on, are really private matters and that government should not be in the business of providing them to the public, given its apparent inability to provide them in efficient and effective ways. Instead, the privilege (or monopoly) to provide such services should be sold off to private companies, which in turn would sell their services to the public for profit. In this way, individuals are encouraged to think of the provision of their basic needs as matters of private preference and private responsibility. Such thinking is reinforced by the popular myth that inequities (in wealth, for instance) result primarily from individuals' diminished capabilities and effort. But it is not the role of government to compensate for these shortcomings. In the New Right account, people want to concentrate on their own lives and those they care about rather than help provide (in a compulsory way) for the well-being of others.

However, the social and economic ramifications of this logic are worrying. For example, it is not hard to imagine that almost all parents want (what they believe to be) the very best for their children, a proposition preyed upon by the New Right. It is understandable, therefore, when parents who are able to do so, remove their children from public schools they perceive to be inadequate and place them in private schools they perceive to be better. What happens to other parents and their children is irrelevant; in a market environment the aim is to act on your own self-interest. In doing so, however, parents advantage their own children at the expense of others (Whitty *et al.* 1998; Thrupp 1999; Labaree 2000). This, in turn, leaves a community with large numbers of young people who have not received the education to help that community prosper or function effectively. What is not appreciated by market discourse, then, is that education is a public good because it benefits not only individuals but also the community of which they are a part (Grace 1989; Marginson 1993; Labaree 2000). Neither is the public interest in education reducible to the sum of the private interests of all individual consumers (Deem *et al.* 1995; Labaree 2000), as neoliberals would have it.

All of us, citizens and non-citizens, including those who send their children to private schools, live with the consequences of public schooling. All of us have a stake in other people being able to vote, work and otherwise live responsible lives and make contributions to the community. Concern for the public good, then, requires that we make judgements about our own lives as they are connected to the lives of others. While *all* children have the right to a good education, individuals can only fully develop themselves when they live and work within a democratic society that recognizes and respects the distinctive contributions each individual has to make (Connell 1993; Ranson 1997). In short, individual identity exists only in association with others; others actually form part of and help to form our identity. Hence, radical democracy depends upon the active participation of those who recognize individualities in a social context as they create the conditions where people can develop both individually and collectively. Reese (1988) provides a similar judgement:

> Democracy is a sham without a system of public schools that introduces everyone to a world of ideas, values, and knowledge that takes all children beyond their own narrow and private worlds ... the public schools must necessarily stand above and in tension with all private concerns. The tension between private visions and public visions will always exist.
>
> (p. 440)

Pressures to make a market economy work in the midst of poverty points to the existence of struggle over conflicting values and interests, which includes competing aims and purposes for education. The social and educational costs of a highly segregated school system with clearly visible social class, racial and ethnic disparities between schools and communities are public problems and require public solutions, yet the resources for public institutions are being seriously eroded.[8] Many urban teachers and administrators are being told that regardless of resources, they have to improve students' academic performance, despite 30 years of empirical evidence that points to the importance of non-school-related factors on students' academic achievement. Nevertheless, 'social context' has been exposed as being too often invoked as an excuse for not educating certain students. Low-income parents have long witnessed how schooling marginalizes and underserves their children when poor academic performance is rationalized in terms of students' home backgrounds. Mounting such arguments, the educational system is excused from its responsibility to educate everyone.

The following comments by a high school principal in our research demonstrate how this dynamic plays itself out in schools; particularly those schools with a history of inadequate funding and academic underachievement and with pressures to improve test scores and meet higher academic standards:

> People learn attitudes from each other, so if someone has low expectations of somebody else, soon the person who it's expected of is going to believe that as well. When youngsters get to high school and they've had folks talking to them about them not being able to learn, by the time they get to high school age they believe it as well. They're liable to say, 'Well, you know what? I don't want to learn that and I don't care.' But it's really a symptom of something else. It's kind of a protection that says, 'I can't do it' . . . that's the way they get away [with it] and then folks believe it. That's why we've got to overcome that.

What to do?

Clearly, better teacher preparation, more efficient school organization and more challenging and engaging curricula are urgently needed in urban areas. Emphasis on student language development, certified bilingual and ESL teachers, qualified teachers who are matched ethnically and by language with their students, and principals who work intensely with teachers, parents and other members of their school's communities can help lift student learning outcomes in public schools (Dentler and Hafner 1997). Yet, disassociating resource allocations, institutional instability, gender, racial and ethnic patterns and other social demographics (such as poverty) from academic achievement, exaggerates what schools can achieve, denies the social limits of education reform and raises false hopes among those trying to improve student outcomes (Grace 1991; Ball 1998; Lauder *et al.* 1999; Thrupp 1999). Because of the influence of contextual variables upon what happens inside schools and classrooms, academic achievement and teacher and administrator problems cannot be fixed by managerialist and technically orientated solutions. Similarly, token forms of parent involvement in schools cannot remedy gaps in school achievement between racial/ethnic student groups nor correct disparities in school conditions. Indeed, as typically constituted, parent involvement schemes – though internationally promoted and containing obvious potential – are more likely to divert attention away from more fundamental economic, social and political problems and the inequalities associated with the rhetoric of 'parental choice' (Gewirtz *et al.* 1995).

The achievement of even modest educational goals, such as significantly increasing high school graduation rates, demands changes in society for a more equitable distribution of wealth, which could mitigate poverty, ignorance, cynicism, racism and sexism. Such large-scale social changes are necessary because gross disparities of power, wealth and income support pervasive inequalities in the provision of schooling. In other words, schooling – its content, processes and organization – embodies the class bias of a market-driven society. This means that all children are not being provided with an equal opportunity to develop their intelligence and realize their potential (Connell 1993). 'Strong' equal opportunity is, among other things, aimed at abolishing inherited 'disprivilege' (Green 1998: 50). It characterizes, for example, a social order in which no one's background is likely to exclude them from the early development of the skills and dispositions necessary for enjoyable, respected and remunerative work.

Extreme inequalities, such as those we have mentioned above, do not come about naturally. Understanding the causes of and possible solutions to worsening inequalities between groups in our societies and their effects on educational outcomes and labour market destinations is a first step toward meaningful discussion and debate over the aims of the 'good' society, education and relations between the two. We are in urgent need of public forums where people at grassroots levels with concerns about the unequal distribution of and access to public resources feel free to voice these concerns. Some schools may wish to make themselves available for such public purposes, providing childcare, refreshments and other necessities to make the forums accessible and inviting. This can be one way to amplify the voices of the excluded and the marginalized in social and economic life (Young 1990). The sharing and use of such knowledge, experience, hopes and frustrations are essential to a democratic and just society. The lesson of many progressive community projects has been and continues to be: when the public is educated and organized, change is possible. The absence of wide-based public deliberation makes it difficult to know how many of us are willing to take steps toward insisting that more funds be allocated to public schools, that all students be engaged in rigorous and meaningful curricula, that all schools be safe schools, that all families drink clean water and so on. 'Social context', in other words, can be used as a basis for collective decision making and community mobilization rather than as an excuse for not educating everyone or for not confronting poverty and racism.

School reform ideas will be long-lasting to the extent that they incorporate a new vision of society. To this end, we need to help one another enlarge our vision of what is possible. One way to do this is to broaden our frame of reference by becoming more familiar with progressive developments in our own locales and elsewhere. For example, where are standards being imposed on corporate behaviour? (See, for example, LeRoy 1997.)

In which cities are low-income residents incorporated into planning and development decisions? (See, for example, LeRoy 1997.) Where has a living/livable wage (versus a minimum wage) campaign been successfully waged? (See, for example, San Jose, Santa Cruz, Los Angeles, California.) Where has business been required to contribute to affordable housing, open-space subsidies and other community benefits? (See, for example, Los Angeles, California.) Where has a basic minimum income been debated? (See, for example, Van Parijs 1992.) Where are there democratic community-accountability schemes that help communities focus on both the state's responsibilities for social services and public institutions as well as on local struggles? Where are students being educated to maintain their mother tongue and also learn a second or even a third language (Corson 1998: 42–82)? Where are teachers helping students discover the joy of making a social contribution? (See the journal *Rethinking Schools*.)[9]

Information, thought, organization and struggle are necessary to realize radical democratic goals. They are also necessary to improve our understanding of the complex forces shaping our lives, those that both further and frustrate progress toward greater democracy and social justice, organization and struggle. Students' education should not be disadvantaged on the basis of where they come from (Brown 1990). Importantly, most students will not benefit from vouchers and charter schools, even those from dominant families (Connell 1993). As we have argued, the increase in various forms of privatization, as they restructure public school systems, encourages greater differences between schools, leading to their unequal funding and resulting in qualitatively different educational experiences for youth (Elmore and Fuller 1996; Walford 1997; Whitty *et al.* 1998; Lauder *et al.* 1999; Thrupp 1999). Yet, recent research suggests that prior achievement and the classed, raced and gendered intake and mix of a school are more crucial to a school's academic success than school organization, management and market sanctions and incentives (Lauder *et al.* 1999). For this reason and because some parents' choices should not be allowed to damage the educational experiences and opportunities of others, we briefly consider proposals for reducing social segregation between schools.

One solution that allows for some parental choice as well as for schools to have a well-balanced social mix is a system of community-mediated choice within a comprehensive or public school system (Lauder *et al.* 1999). In such a scheme, parents would be able to list their school preferences but the community, as expressed through local government, would have the responsibility of reconciling parents' preferences in order to achieve well-balanced intakes in all schools (Lauder *et al.* 1999: 136). Similarly, Walford (1997: 64) argues that all families should be required to select three or four schools in order of preference. When parents cannot get their first preference due to a school being oversubscribed, applications would be randomly selected. His plan includes procedures for making funding, information and transportation available to families. A second and similar solution is posed by Thrupp who has carefully examined class-based resistance and its possible implications for measures that would spread both poverty and resources throughout schools more evenly. While concluding that the power of the state is necessary to 'temper the aspirations of the powerful and protect those who are less influential and well-resourced' (1999: 184), Thrupp also acknowledges that in the current political climate, state intervention may not be feasible. Nevertheless, were it to become so, he asks, what could we do? His suggestions include reconsidering the use of residential segregation as the basis for school enrolment, using balloting or zoning to ensure that schools have a reasonable mix of students, and regulated choice schemes. The concern behind these schemes is that as long as schools are threatened by privileged parents who can, when dissatisfied, easily remove their children from one school to place them in another, schools will be forced to choose between equity-based reforms and losing from their schools those parents with access to scarce economic and cultural capital (Stuart Wells and Serna 1996).

During the 1980s and 1990s, the state has lost credibility as a force for social betterment or even responding to people's needs. Private market criteria for efficiency and success have been embraced by people across the political spectrum in response to failings of the post-war welfare state and economic management. Neoliberal policies – which call for increased privatization of schools, choice, and vouchers, for example – have redefined what counts as democracy so that it now guarantees choice (for a few) in an 'unfettered' market (Apple 2000: 67). Yet, increasing social divisions and forms of inequality, un- and underemployment, public loss of confidence in public institutions, and the brief record of marketization in Eastern Europe, suggest that the market may not be able to satisfy human needs. This, then, raises the following questions: if markets were not the prime regulator of the economy, what could be? Is it possible to democratize economic life? Is poverty an issue for social policy or is it an inevitable product of natural laws? In order to seriously ponder these challenges we must, as a first condition, recognize that the differences and similarities between others and ourselves are, or can be, starting points for new solidarities and new alliances (McCarthy and Dimitriades 2000). In addition to providing vehicles through which we can directly confront the sources of exclusion and marginalization, such alliances can also inform teachers' and administrators' efforts to draw on diverse communities as sources of inspiration for both pedagogy and school organization (Gale and Densmore 2000). We must also recognize that in order to have full democracy, the needs of the many would have to outweigh the power of the few.

Conclusion

The market discourse that currently dominates what we (are supposed to) think about education includes the illusion that it is largely a private benefit, even though business and government are actively involved in publicly espousing and influencing what kind of education students should receive. That is, while governments are retreating from putting resources into the public domain, it is not so clear that their influence is similarly diminishing. Embedded within this contradictory discourse is also the paradox that how disadvantaged students fare in school is predominantly their own responsibility, irrespective of the social and economic inequalities that generate these outcomes. Of course, these do not need to be the only public and private thoughts in relation to schooling. Most teachers try to do their best in often difficult circumstances. Many of their circumstances are outside their direct control; they are often as much victims as their students. But while teachers can easily feel overwhelmed by the enormity of the problems they face, they can still have a positive influence on the present and future lives of their students.

This positive influence, we believe, should be broadly informed by viewing education as a public issue, not simply a private matter. We must reconnect school and society in ways other than those intended by the market and neoliberalism so that social division is undermined and social justice is promoted. Two ways in which this can be achieved at the school and classroom level are by: (1) positioning communities as integral to the curricula (not redundant or even antagonistic to it), and by (2) recognizing community members as knowledgeable about their communities, as valid bearers of knowledge about their world and as needed representatives of diverse groups with responsibilities to both schools as well as their constituencies.

This repositioning of community means a different kind of role for teachers as political activists in communities, not as powerless bystanders. In dialogue with diverse community members, teachers would explore different ways in which they can be a part of their schools' communities. This would include learning what 'high expectations', 'self-respect', 'achievement' and 'leadership' mean for different cultures and how these values could be supported in classrooms. As teachers learn about the textures of their students' lives, they will better know how to expand democracy by promoting respect for diverse cultures, including those both within and outside their schools. To end where we began this book, teachers clearly have valuable skills and knowledge that schools and their communities need, but they do not have all that is needed. Working with and amongst communities, learning from them, teachers are better placed to make valuable contributions to the education of students and to a radical democratic agenda for western societies.

Questions for discussion/research

- Is democracy best conceived of as an end or as a means?
- How might greater democracy in society affect educational possibilities?
- How can the democratization of schooling be used to promote social justice in society?

- How would improving social mix affect a school's curriculum and/or a teacher's pedagogy?

Suggested readings

Barber, B. (1984) *Strong Democracy, Participatory Politics for a New Age*. Berkeley: University of California Press, Chapter 9.

Brantlinger, E. (1993) *The Politics of Social Class in Secondary School*. New York: Teachers College Press, Chapter 8.

Orfield, G., Eaton, S.E. and the Harvard Project on School Desegregation (1996) *Dismantling Desegregation*. New York: New Press, Chapter 12.

Perrucci, R. and Wysong, E. (1999) *The New Class Society*. Boulder, CO: Rowman & Littlefield Publishers, Chapters 6 and 8.

Young, I.M. (1990) *Justice and the Politics of Difference*. Princeton, NJ: Princeton University Press, Chapter 8.

Notes

1 Introduction

1 Space does not permit a more comprehensive critique of Lummis' (1996) conception of *people* power. Suffice to say, people are not homogeneous although we do not consider stretching heterogeneity all the way to an atomized individualism (see Chapter 4) as *just* democracy. It is in our critical natures, then, to want both in a radical account of democracy; people groups or people*s* is an important position to hold with regard to social justice (see Gale and Densmore 2000).
2 After Sayer (1995: ix), 'radical' here signals a critique of the political economy of the likes of Adam Smith and John Stuart Mill, a critique that was also intended by Marx. Radical political economy is also a self-reflexive critique.

2 Markets

1 See Sayers (1992) for an excellent assessment of the virtues of the market.
2 For a discussion of the apparent tensions between equity, efficiency and effectiveness in the Australian university sector during the 1990s, see Gale and McNamee (1994).
3 See Peters *et al.* (2000) for one review of relevant work in this area.
4 For a brilliant explication and analysis of group representation, see Iris Marion Young (1990). See also Gale and Densmore (2000) for a discussion of discourses of difference in education.
5 See Chapter 3 for a discussion of teachers' engagement with standardized testing.
6 See Young (1990), especially Chapter 8, for her discussion of the problems with local autonomy, the ideal of 'community', and possibilities for the organization of public life. Also, see Henig *et al.* (1999) for analyses of education reform in relation to civic capacity in cities in the United States of America.

3 Policy

1 We are indebted to Colin Lankshear for acquainting us with de Certeau's (1984) work from which we realized the potential for a policy analysis of 'uses' and 'tactics'.
2 We admit to some slippage here and elsewhere in this monograph in referring to the state and government. In fact, they are different concepts supported by their

own bodies of literature and present different implications for policy production. Hoffman (1995) provides a good account of such distinctions and the need for them. However, these discussions are beyond the scope and primary interest of this chapter.

3 Chapters 2 and 5 for a more detailed discussion of these issues of marketization and professionalism.

4 Note the similarities here with the starfish analogy in Chapter 1.

5 Ball's (1994a: 19) references above to teachers' 'productive thought, invention and adaptation' in response to policy provide an exception, although in place/space distinctions this still seems to be reactive rather than proactive and not always clearly delineated.

6 This in itself is illustrative of the tactics and uses we employ as policy analysts.

7 Dale's (1989) reference to policy strategies and tactics provides an exception to this and is worth reconsidering.

4 Leadership

1 On this point, see the discussion on radical democracy in Chapter 1 and policy production in Chapter 3.

2 It is worth comparing these with the interests of our socially critical disposition in Chapter 1.

3 For an analysis of the poor fit between credentials and job requirements or job performance, see Hacker (1997), Chapter 11.

4 We are grateful to Douglas Tsang for introducing us to these Chinese characters and their meanings.

5 Professionalism

1 See Gale (2002) for a critique of this account of students' learning in Australian higher education settings.

2 Primary/elementary teachers often see themselves (favourably) as involved in the former and their secondary counterparts as involved in the latter.

3 It is this domination by teachers and teacher-educators of what is considered valuable knowledge for professional teachers that has served as a point of dissension for other interests, which claim that the profession is out of touch with what society and the economy now needs from its teachers.

4 See Lisa Delpit's (1996) critique of the unmitigated use of process-centred approaches to teaching low-income African-American students how to read and write.

6 Community

1 See Ira Katznelson and Margaret Weir (1985) for a discussion of public education as the guardian of a democratic and egalitarian culture in the United States.

2 For different views on this subject see Foster (1993), Kozol (1993), Orfield *et al.* (1996), Thrupp (1999) and West (1990).

3 These are processes with some similarities to the three conditions of recognitive justice, which we have written about elsewhere (Gale and Densmore 2000).

4 See Gale (2001b, 2002) for a more detailed discussion on issues of time and space in relation to students' academic achievement.

5 For further discussion on these issues, see Benn (1997), Walford (1994), Kozol (1991), Orfield *et al.* (1996) and Waslander and Thrupp (1995, in Thrupp 1999: 185–9).

6 For a more thorough explication and analysis, see Lauder (1991), Lauder and Hughes (1990) and Gale and Densmore (2000).

7 See Chapter 3 for a discussion of the relative power of teachers as policy 'consumers'.

8 See Kozol (1991) for an indictment of the existing inequalities between schools in the United States.

9 *Rethinking Schools* (www.rethinkingschools.org (accessed 16 January 2003)) is an excellent journal for learning about progressive teaching practices and challenges in education, covering a wide range of educational issues.

References

Agger, B. (1998) *Critical Social Theories: An Introduction.* Boulder, CO: Westview.

Althusser, L. (1969) *For Marx.* Harmondsworth: Penguin.

Anderson, J.E. (1979) *Public Policy Making* (2nd edn). New York: Holt, Rinehart & Winston.

Anyon, J. (1981) Social class and school knowledge, *Curriculum Inquiry,* 11(1): 3–42.

Anyon, J. (1997) *Ghetto Schooling: A Political Economy of Urban Educational Reform.* New York: Teachers College Press.

Apple, M. (1986) *Teachers and Texts: A Political Economy of Class and Gender Relations in Education.* Boston, MA: Routledge and Kegan Paul.

Apple, M.W. (2000) Between neoliberalism and neoconservatism: education and conservatism in a global context, in N.C. Burbules and C.A. Torres (eds) *Globalization and Education, Critical Perspectives.* New York: Routledge.

Aronowitz, S. (1997) Between nationality and class, *Harvard Educational Review,* 67: 188–207.

Balfanz, R. (2000) Why do so many urban public school students demonstrate so little academic achievement?, in M. Sanders (ed.) *Schooling Students Placed at Risk: Research, Policy, and Practice in the Education of Poor and Minority Adolescents.* Mahwah, NJ: LEA.

Ball, S. (1988) Staff relations during the teachers' industrial action: context, conflict and proletarianisation, *British Journal of Sociology of Education,* 9(3): 289–306.

Ball, S. (1990) *Politics and Policy Making in Education: Explorations in Policy Sociology.* London: Routledge.

Ball, S. (1993) Education markets, choice and social class: the market as a class strategy in the UK and US, *British Journal of Sociology of Education,* 14(1): 3–19.

Ball, S. (1994a) *Education Reform: A Critical and Post-Structural Approach.* Buckingham: Open University Press.

Ball, S. (1994b) Researching inside the State: issues in the interpretation of elite interviews, in D. Halpin and B. Troyna (eds) *Researching Education Policy: Ethical and Methodological Issues.* London: Falmer Press.

Ball, S. (1997) Policy sociology and critical social research: a personal view of recent education policy and policy research, *British Educational Research Journal,* 23(1): 257–74.

Ball, S. (1998) Educational studies, policy entrepreneurship and social theory, in R. Slee, G. Weiner with S. Tomlinson (eds) *School Effectiveness for Whom? Challenges to the School Effectiveness and School Improvement Movements.* London: Falmer Press.

Ball, S. (1999) *Global Trends in Educational Reform and the Struggle for the Soul of the Teacher.* London: Centre for Public Policy Research, King's College.

Barber, B. (1965) Some problems in the sociology of the professions, *Daedalus*, 92: 669–88.

Barber, B. (1984) *Strong Democracy: Participatory Politics for a New Age*. Berkeley: University of California Press.

Baudrillard, J. (1981) *For a Critique of the Political Economy of the Sign* (trans. C. Levin). St Louis, MO: Telos Press.

Bell, J. and Harrison, B. (1998) *Leading People: Learning from People: Lessons from Education Professionals*. Buckingham: Open University Press.

Benn, C. (1997) Effective comprehensive education, in R. Pring and G. Walford (eds) *Affirming the Comprehensive Ideal*. London: Falmer Press.

Bidwell, C. (1965) The school as a formal organization, in J.G. March (ed.) *Handbook of Organizations*. Chicago: Rand-McNally.

Blackmore, J. (1990) School-based decision-making and teacher unions: the appropriation of a discourse, in J. Chapman (ed.) *School-Based Decision-Making and Management*. London: Falmer Press.

Bottery, M. (1992) *The Ethics of Educational Management: Personal, Social and Political Perspectives on School Organization*. London: Cassell.

Bourdieu, P. (1997) The forms of capital, in A. Halsey, H. Lauder, P. Brown and A. Stuart Wells (eds) *Education: Culture, Economy and Society*. Oxford: Oxford University Press.

Bourdieu, P. and Wacquant, L. (1992) *An Invitation to Reflexive Sociology*. Cambridge: Polity Press.

Bowe, R., Ball, S. and Gold, A. (1992) *Reforming Education and Changing Schools: Case Studies in Policy Sociology*. London: Routledge.

Bowles, S. and Gintis, H. (1976) *Schooling in Capitalist America*. New York: Basic.

Brantlinger, E.A. (1993) *The Politics of Social Class in Secondary School: Views of Affluent and Impoverished Youth*. New York: Teachers College Press.

Brighouse, H. (2000) *School Choice and Social Justice*. New York: Oxford University Press.

Brint, S. (1998) *Schools and Societies*. Thousand Oaks, CA: Pine Forge Press.

Brooks, S. (2000) Poverty and environmentally induced damage to children, in V. Polakow (ed.) *The Public Assault on America's Children: Poverty, Violence and Juvenile Injustice*. New York: Teachers College Press.

Brown, P. (1990) The Third Wave: education and the ideology of parentocracy, *British Journal of Sociology of Education*, 11(1): 65–85.

Brown, P. (1995) Cultural capital and social exclusion: some observations on recent trends in education, employment and the labour market, in A. Halsey, H. Lauder, P. Brown and A. Stuart Wells (eds) *Education, Culture, Economy, Society*. Oxford: Oxford University Press.

Brown, P., Halsey, A., Lauder, H. and Stuart Wells, A. (1997) The transformation of education and society: an introduction, in A. Halsey, H. Lauder, P. Brown and A. Stuart Wells (eds) *Education: Culture, Economy and Society*. Oxford: Oxford University Press.

Buchanan, I. (1993) Extraordinary spaces in ordinary places: de Certeau and the space of post-colonialism, *SPAN 36* (http://www.mcc.murdoch.edu.au/ReadingRoom/litserv/SPAN/36/Jabba.html (accessed 4 December 2000)).

Burbules, N. (1997) Why practice doesn't make perfect: the pragmatics of teaching knowledge. Paper presented at the 27th Annual Conference of the Australian Teacher Education Association, 'Diversity, Difference & Discontinuity: (Re)mapping teacher education for the next decade', Yeppoon, Queensland, Australia, 5–8 July.

Burbules, N.C. and Densmore, K. (1991) The limits of making teaching a profession, *Educational Policy*, 5(1): 44–63.

Caldwell, B. (1998) *Self-Managing Schools and Improved Learning Outcomes*. Canberra: DEETYA.

Caldwell, B. and Spinks, J. (1988) *The Self-Managing School*. London: Falmer Press.

Carspecken, P. (1996) *Critical Ethnography in Educational Research: A Theoretical and Practical Guide*. New York: Routledge.

Chubb, J. and Moe, T. (1990) *Politics, Markets and America's Schools*. Washington, DC: Brookings Institute.

Clarke, J., Cochrane, A. and McLaughlin, E. (eds) (1994) *Managing Social Policy*. London: Sage.

Coady, T. (ed.) (2000) *Why Universities Matter: A Conversation About Values, Means and Directions*. St Leonards, NSW: Allen & Unwin.

Colebatch, H. (1998) *Policy*. Buckingham: Open University Press.

Connell, R. (1994) Poverty and education, *Harvard Educational Review*, 64(2): 125–49.

Connell, R., Ashenden, D., Kessler, S. and Dowsett, G. (1982) *Making the Difference: Schools, Families and Social Division*. Sydney: Allen & Unwin.

Connell, R.W. (1993) *Schools and Social Justice*. Sydney: Pluto Press.

Considine, M. (1988) The corporate management framework as administrative practice: a critique, *Journal of Public Administration*, 47(1): 4–18.

Corson, D. (1998) *Changing Education for Diversity*. Buckingham: Open University Press.

Cunningham, F. (1987) *Democratic Theory and Socialism*. Cambridge: Cambridge University Press.

Dale, R. (1989) *The State and Education Policy*. Milton Keynes: Open University Press.

Dale, R. (1992) Whither the State and education policy? Recent work in Australia and New Zealand, *British Journal of Sociology of Education*, 13(3): 387–95.

Dale, R. and Ozga, J. (1993) Two hemispheres, both New Right? 1980s education reforms in New Zealand and Wales, in R. Lingard, J. Knight and P. Porter (eds) *Schooling Reform in Hard Times*. London: Falmer Press.

Danaher, P., Gale, T. and Erben, T. (2000) The teacher educator as (re)negotiated professional: critical incidents in steering between State and market, *International Journal of Education for Teaching*, 26(1): 55–71.

Darden, J.T., Dunleep, H.O. and Glaster, G.C. (1992) Civil rights in metropolitan America, *Journal of Urban Affairs*, 14: 469–96.

de Certeau, M. (1984) *The Practice of Everyday Life* (Vol. 1). Berkeley, CA: University of California Press.

Deem, R., Brehony, K. and Heath, S. (1995) *Active Citizenship and the Governing of Schools*. Buckingham: Open University Press.

Deever, B. (1996) Is this radical enough? Curriculum reform, change and the language of probability, *Interchange*, 27(3 & 4): 251–60.

Delpit, L. (1996) The politics of teaching literate discourse, in W. Ayers and P. Ford (eds) *City Kids, City Teachers*. New York: New Press.

Dentler, R. and Hafner, A. (1997) *Hosting Newcomers, Structuring Educational Opportunities for Immigrant Children*. New York: Teachers College Press.

Dewey, J. (1958) *Philosophy of Education: Problems of Men*. Totowa, NJ: Littlefield, Adams.

Dewey, J. ([1916] 1966) *Democracy and Education: An Introduction to the Philosophy of Education*. New York: Free Press.

Easton, D. (1953) *The Political System*. New York: Alfred A. Knopf.

Elmore, R.F. and Fuller, B. (1996) Empirical research on educational choice: what are the implications for policymakers?, in B. Fuller, R.F. Elmore and G. Orfield (eds) *Who Chooses, Who Loses? Culture, Institutions and the Unequal Effects of School Choice*. New York: Teachers College Press.

Epstein, J. (1984) Effects of teacher practices and parent involvement on student achievement. Paper presented at the American Educational Research Association Conference, New Orleans, April.

Foster, M. (1993) 'Savage inequalities': where have we come from? Where are we going? *Educational Theory*, 43: 23–32.

Foster, W. (1989) Toward a critical practice of leadership, in J. Smyth (ed.) *Critical Perspectives on Educational Leadership*. London: Falmer Press.

Foucault, M. (1972) *The Archaeology of Knowledge*. London: Tavistock.

Foucault, M. (1977) *Discipline and Punish: The Birth of the Prison*. London: Penguin.

Franklin, W. (2000) Students at promise and resilient: a historical look at risk, in M. Sanders (ed.) *Schooling Students Placed at Risk: Research, Policy and Practice in the Education of Poor and Minority Adolescents*. Mahwah, NJ: LEA.

Fraser, N. (1997) *Justice Interruptus: Critical Reflections on the 'Post-Socialist' Condition*. New York: Routledge.

Freeland, J. (1986) Australia: the search for a new educational settlement, in R. Sharp (ed.) *Capitalist Crisis and Schooling: Comparative Studies in the Politics of Education*. Melbourne: Macmillan.

Freeman, R. (1995) The limits of wage flexibility to curing unemployment, *Oxford Review of Economic Policy*, 11(1): 63–72.

Freire, P. (1972) *Pedagogy of the Oppressed*. Harmondsworth: Penguin.

Fullan, M. and Hargreaves, A. (1996) *What's Worth Fighting for in Your School* (2nd edn). New York: Teachers College Press.

Furlong, J., Barton, L., Miles, S., Whiting, C. and Whitty, G. (2000) *Teacher Education in Transition: Re-Forming Professionalism?* Buckingham: Open University Press.

Gale, T. (1994) Story-telling and policy making: the construction of university entrance problems in Australia, *Journal of Education Policy*, 9(3): 227–32.

Gale, T. (1997) Vocality in policy production: excavations of Australian higher education policy. Paper presented at the Australian Association for Research in Education (AARE) Conference, Brisbane, Australia, 30 November–4 December.

Gale, T. (1999a) Fair contest or elite sponsorship? Entry settlements in Australian higher education, *Higher Education Policy*, 12(1): 69–91.

Gale, T. (1999b) Policy trajectories: treading the discursive path of policy analysis, *Discourse: Studies in the Cultural Politics of Education*, 20(3): 393–407.

Gale, T. (2000) Putting academics in their place, *Australian Educational Researcher*, 27(2): 121–36.

Gale, T. (2001a) Critical policy sociology: historiography, archaeology and genealogy as methods of policy analysis, *Journal of Education Policy*, 16(5): 379–93.

Gale, T. (2001b) To speak of academic achievement and justice: a dialogue of time and place for students and their schooling, *Teaching Education*, 12(3): 371–80.

Gale, T. (2002) Degrees of difficulty: an ecological account of learning in Australian higher education, *Studies in Higher Education*, 27(1): 65–78.

Gale, T. (2003) Realizing policy: the who and how of policy production, *Discourse*.

Gale, T. and Densmore, K. (2000) *Just Schooling: Explorations in the Cultural Politics of Teaching*. Buckingham: Open University Press.

Gale, T. and McNamee, P. (1994) Just out of reach: access to equity in Australian higher education, *The Australian Universities' Review*, 37(2): 8–12.

Gale, T. and McNamee, P. (1995) Alternative pathways to traditional destinations: higher education for disadvantaged Australians, *British Journal of Sociology of Education*, 16(4): 437–50.

Gale, T.C. and Jackson, C. (1997) Preparing professionals: student-teachers and their supervisors at work, *Asia-Pacific Journal of Teacher Education*, 25(2): 177–91.

Gee, J., Hull, G. and Lankshear, C. (1996) *The New Work Order: Behind the Language of the New Capitalism*. Boulder, CO: Westview Press.

Gewirtz, S., Ball, S. and Bowe, R. (1995) *Markets, Choice and Equity in Education*. Buckingham: Open University Press.

Giddens, A. (1994) *Beyond Left and Right: The Future of Radical Politics*. Cambridge: Cambridge University Press.

Gillborn, D. and Youdell, D. (2000) *Rationing Education, Policy, Practice, Reform and Equity*. Buckingham: Open University Press.

Glatter, R., Woods, P.A. and Bagley, C. (eds) (1997) *Choice and Diversity in Schooling, Perspectives and Prospects*. London: Routledge.

Gordon, I., Lewis, J. and Young, K. (1977) Perspectives on policy analysis, *Public Administration Bulletin*, 25: 26–35.

Gore, J. (1998) Disciplining bodies: on the continuity of power relations in pedagogy, in T. Popkewitz and M. Brennan (eds) *Foucault's Challenge: Discourse, Knowledge, and Power in Education*. New York: Teachers College Press.

Gorz, A. (1992) On the difference between society and community, and why basic income cannot by itself confer full membership of either, in P. Van Parijs (ed.) *Arguing for Basic Income, Ethical Foundations for a Radical Reform*. London: Verso.

Grace, G. (1978) *Teachers, Ideology and Control: A Study in Urban Education*. London: Routledge and Kegan Paul.

Grace, G. (1989) Education: commodity or public good?, *British Journal of Educational Studies*, 37(3): 207–21.

Grace, G. (1991) Welfare Labourism versus the New Right: the struggle in New Zealand's education policy, *International Studies in Sociology of Education*, 1(1): 25–42.

Grace, G. (1994) Education is a public good: on the need to resist the domination of economic science, in D. Bridges and T. McLaughlin (eds) *Education and the Market Place*. London: Falmer Press.

Grace, G. (1995) *School Leadership: Beyond Education Management, an Essay in Policy Scholarship*. London: Falmer Press.

Green, P. (1998) *Equality and Democracy*. New York: The New Press.

Greenwood, E. (1957) Attributes of a profession, *Social Work*, 2–3 July: 45–55.

Grimmett, P. and Neufeld, J. (eds) (1994) *Teacher Development and the Struggle for Authenticity: Professional Growth and Restructuring in the Context of Change*. New York: Teachers College Press.

Hacker, A. (1997) *Money: Who Has How Much and Why*. New York: Scribner.

Hancock, L. (ed.) (1999) *Women, Public Policy and the State*. London: MacMillan.

Hargreaves, A. and Evans, R. (eds) (1997) *Beyond Educational Reform: Bringing Teachers Back*. Buckingham: Open University Press.

Hatcher, R. (1994) Market relationships and the management of teachers, *British Journal of Sociology of Education*, 15(1): 41–61.

Hatcher, R. (1996) The limitations of the new social democratic agendas: class, equality and agency, in R. Hatcher, K. Jones, B. Regan and C. Richards (eds) *Education Under the Conservatives*. Stoke-on-Trent: Trentham Books.

Heclo, H. (1978) Issues networks and the executive establishment, in A. King (ed.) *The New American Political System*. Washington, DC: American Enterprise Institute.

Heelas, P. and Morris, P. (eds) (1992) *The Values of the Enterprise Culture: The Moral Debate*. London: Routledge.

Helsby, G. (1999) *Changing Teachers' Work*. Buckingham: Open University Press.

Henig, J., Hula, R., Orr, M. and Pedescleaux, D. (1999) *The Color of School Reform, Race, Politics and the Challenge of Urban Education*. Princeton, NJ: Princeton University Press.

Henry, M. (1992) Higher education for all? Tensions and contradictions in post-compulsory and higher education policy in Australia, *Journal of Education Policy*, 7(4): 399–413.

Henry, M. (1993) What is policy? A response to Stephen Ball, *Discourse*, 14(1): 102–5.

Henry, M., Knight, J., Lingard, R. and Taylor, S. (1988) *Understanding Schooling: An Introductory Sociology of Australian Education*. London: Routledge.

Herrnstein, R.J. and Murray, C. (1994) *The Bell Curve: Intelligence and Class Structure in American Life*. New York: The Free Press.

Hoffman, J. (1995) *Beyond the State: An Introductory Critique*. Cambridge: Polity Press.

Howsam, R., Corrigan, D., Denemark, G. and Nash, R. (1976) *Educating a Profession: A Report of the Bicentennial Commission on Education for the Profession of Teaching*. Washington, DC: AACTE.

Hoyle, E. (1982) The professionalization of teachers: a paradox, *British Journal of Educational Studies*, 30(2): 61–71.

Jameson, F. (1983) Postmodernism and consumer society, in H. Foster (ed.) *Postmodern Culture*. London: Pluto Books.

Johnson, T. (1972) *Professions and Power*. London: Macmillan.

Karp, S. (2002) Let them eat tests, *Rethinking Schools*, 16, summer: 3, 4, 23.

Katznelson, I. and Weir, M. (1985) *Schooling for All, Class, Race and the Decline of the Democratic Ideal*. New York: Basic Books.

Keating, M. and Davis, G. (eds) (2000) *The Future of Governance*. St Leonards, NSW: Allen & Unwin.

Kenway, J. (1990) *Gender and Education Policy: A Call for New Directions*. Geelong: Deakin University Press.

Kickert, W. (1991) Steering at a distance: a new paradigm of public governance in Dutch higher education. Paper presented at the European Consortium for Political Research Conference, University of Essex, March.

Kincheloe, J. and McLaren, P. (1994) Rethinking critical theory and qualitative research, in N. Denzin and Y. Lincoln (eds) *Handbook of Qualitative Research*. London: Sage.

Kincheloe, J. and Steinberg, S. (1997) *Changing Multiculturalism*. Buckingham: Open University Press.

Knight, T. (1998) Public education: Northland Secondary College versus the State, *International Journal of Inclusive Education*, 2(4): 295–308.

Kozol, J. (1991) *Savage Inequalities*. New York: Crown Publishing.

Kozol, J. (1993) Savage inequalities: an interview with Jonathan Kozol, *Educational Theory*, 43: 55–70.

Kozol, J. (1995) *Amazing Grace: The Lives of Children and the Conscience of a Nation*. New York: Harper Collins.

Labaree, D. (1992) Power, knowledge and the rationalization of teaching: a genealogy of the movement to professionalize teaching, *Harvard Educational Review*, 62(2): 123–54.

Labaree, D. (1997) Public goods, private goods: the American struggle over educational goals, *American Educational Research Journal*, 34(1): 39–81.

Labaree, D.F. (2000) No exit: public education as an inescapably public good, in L. Cuban and D. Shipps (eds) *Reconstructing the Common Good in Education, Coping with Intractable American Dilemmas*. Stanford, CA: Stanford University Press.

124   *Engaging teachers*

Laclau, E. and Mouffe, C. (2001) *Hegemony and Socialist Strategy: Towards a Radical Democratic Politics* (2nd edn). London: Verso.
Lankshear, C. (2002) Steps towards a pedagogy of tactics. Paper presented at the Faculty of Education Seminar Series, Monash University, Clayton, Australia, 26 June.
Lareau, A. (1987) Social-class differences in family–school relationships: the importance of cultural capital, *Sociology of Education*, 60: 73–85.
Lareau, A. (1989) *Home Advantage*. New York: Falmer Press.
Larson, M. (1977) *The Rise of Professionalism: A Sociological Analysis*. Berkeley, CA: University of California Press.
Lauder, H. (1990) Education, democracy and the crisis of the Welfare State, in H. Lauder and C. Wylie (eds) *Towards Successful Schooling*. London: Falmer.
Lauder, H. (1991) Education, democracy and the economy, *British Journal of Sociology of Education*, 12: 417–31.
Lauder, H. and Hughes, D. (1990) Social inequalities and differences in school outcomes, *New Zealand Journal of Educational Studies*, 25: 37–60.
Lauder, H., Hughes, D., Watson, S., et al. (1995) *Trading in Futures: The Nature of Choice in Educational Markets in New Zealand*. Wellington: Ministry of Education.
Lauder, H., Hughes, D., Watson, S., et al. (1999) *Trading in Futures: Why Markets in Education Don't Work*. Buckingham: Open University Press.
Lauder, H., Jamieson, I. and Wikeley, F. (1998) Models of effective schools: limits and capabilities, in R. Slee, G. Weiner with S. Tomlinson (eds) *School Effectiveness for Whom? Challenges to the School Effectiveness and School Improvement Movements*. London: Falmer Press.
Lauder, H. and Wylie, C. (1990) *Towards Successful Schooling*. London: Falmer Press.
Lawn, M. (1996) *Modern Times? Work, Professionalism and Citizenship in Teaching*. London: Falmer Press.
Lawn, M. and Ozga, J. (1988) The educational worker? A reassessment of teachers, in J. Ozga (ed.) *Schoolwork: Approaches to the Labour Processes of Teaching*. Milton Keynes: Open University Press.
Lawton, D. (1986) The Department of Education and Science: policy-making at the centre, in A. Hartnett and M. Naish (eds) *Education and Society Today*. Lewes: Falmer Press.
Leithwood, K., Jantzi, D. and Steinbach, R. (1999) *Changing Leadership for Changing Times*. Buckingham: Open University Press.
LeRoy, G. (1997) *No More Candy Store: States and Cities Making Job Subsidies Accountable*. Washington, DC: The Institute on Taxation and Economic Policy.
Levitas, R. (1996) The concept of social exclusion and the new Durkheimian hegemony, *Critical Social Policy*, 16(46): 5–20.
Limerick, B. and Lingard, B. (1995) *Gender and Changing Educational Management*. Sydney: Hodder Education.
Lingard, B. and Garrick, B. (1997) Producing and practising social justice policy in education: a policy trajectory study from Queensland, Australia, *International Journal in Sociology of Education*, 7(2): 157–79.
Lingard, B., Hayes, D. and Mills, M. (2002) Developments in school-based management: the specific case of Queensland, Australia, *Journal of Educational Administration*, 40(1): 6–30.
Lingard, B., Mills, M. and Hayes, D. (2000) Teachers, school reform and social justice: challenging research and practice, *Australian Educational Researcher*, 27(3): 99–116.

Lively, D.E. (1994) The diminishing relevance of rights: racial disparities in the distribution of lead exposure risks, *Boston College Environmental Affairs Law Review*, 21(2): 309–34.

Lummis, C.D. (1996) *Radical Democracy*. Ithaca, NY: Cornell University Press.

Lyotard, J. (1984) *The Postmodern Condition: A Report on Knowledge* (trans. G. Bennington and B. Massumi). Manchester: Manchester University Press.

Mac An Ghaill, M. (1992) Teachers' work: curriculum restructuring, culture, power and comprehensive schooling, *British Journal of Sociology of Education*, 13(2): 177–200.

Mac An Ghaill, M. (1994) *The Making of Men: Masculinities, Sexualities and Schooling*. Buckingham: Open University Press.

Malone, K. (1999a) Environmental education researchers as environmental activists, *Environmental Education Research*, 5(2): 163–77.

Malone, K. (1999b) Reclaiming silenced voices through practices of education and environmental popular knowledge production, *Canadian Journal of Environmental Education*, 4(summer): 231–42.

Malone, K. and Walker, R. (1999) Crafting counter-narrative in collaboration: an impressionist tale about a school and community in crisis, *Advances in Program Evaluation*, 6: 191–213.

Marceau, J. (1993) *Steering from a Distance: International Trends in the Financing and Governance of Higher Education*. Canberra: AGPS.

Marginson, S. (1993) *Education and Public Policy in Australia*. Cambridge: Cambridge University Press.

Marginson, S. (1997) *Markets in Education*. St. Leonards, NSW: Allen & Unwin.

Martin, R., McCollow, McFarlane, L., *et al.* (eds) (1994) *Devolution, Decentralisation and Recentralisation: The Structure of Australian Schooling*. Melbourne: Australian Education Union.

McCarthy, C. (1997) Nonsynchrony and social difference: an alternative to current radical accounts of race and schooling, in A. Halsey, H. Lauder, P. Brown and A. Stuart Wells (eds) *Education: Culture, Economy and Society*. Oxford: Oxford University Press.

McCarthy, C. and Dimitriades, G. (2000) Globalizing pedagogies: power, resentment and the renarration of difference, in N.C. Burbules and C.A. Torres (eds) *Globalization and Education, Critical Perspectives*. New York: Routledge.

McPherson, A. and Willms, D. (1987) Equalisation and improvement: some effects of comprehensive reorganisation in Scotland, *Sociology*, 21: 509–39.

Metz, M. (1990) How social class differences shape teachers' work, in M.W. McLaughlin, J.E. Talbert and N. Bascia (eds) *The Context of Teaching in Secondary Schools*. New York: Teachers College Press.

Mills, C. and Gale, T. (2002) Schooling and the (re)production of social inequalities: what can and should we be doing?, *Melbourne Studies in Education*, 43(1): 107–28.

Mills, C.W. (1959) *The Sociological Imagination*. Oxford: Oxford University Press.

Moore, D. and Davenport, S. (1990) Choice: the new improved sorting machine, in W. Boyd and H. Walberg (eds) *Choice in Education: Potential and Problems*. Berkeley, CA: McCutchan.

Moses, R.P., Cobb, C.E. and Cobb Jr, C.E. (2001) *Radical Equations: Math Literacy and Civil Rights*. Boston: Beacon Press.

Newman and Associates, F. (1996) *Authentic Achievement: Restructuring Schools for Intellectual Quality*. San Francisco: Jossey Bass.

Nieto, S. (ed.) (2000) *Puerto Rican Students in US Schools*. Mahwah, NJ: LEA.

Novak, M. (1982) *The Spirit of Democratic Capitalism*. New York: American Enterprise Institute, Simon and Schuster.

Offe, C. (1984) *Contradictions of the Welfare State*. Cambridge, MA: MIT Press.

Offe, C. (1985) *Disorganised Capitalism: Contemporary Transformations of Work and Politics*. Cambridge: Polity Press.

Olsen, L. (2001) From here to equity, the new California school accountability system, *California Tomorrow, Creating a Fair and Equitable Society for Everyone*, Newsletter (Spring): 8–10.

Orfield, G., Eaton, S.E. and the Harvard Project on School Desegregation (1996) *Dismantling Desegregation*. New York: New York Press.

Ozga, J.T. (1990) Policy research and policy theory: a comment on Fitz and Halpin, *Journal of Education Policy*, 5: 359–62.

Ozga, J.T. and Lawn, M. (1981) *Teachers, Professionalism and Class*. Lewes: Falmer Press.

Parekh, B. (1986) The concept of multi-cultural education, in S. Modgil, G. Verma, K. Mallick and C. Modgil (eds) *Multicultural Education: The Interminable Debate*. London: Falmer Press.

Perrucci, R. and Wysong, E. (1999) *The New Class Society*. Boulder, CO: Rowman & Littlefield Publishers Inc.

Peshkin, A. (2001) *Permissible Advantage? The Moral Consequences of Elite Schooling*. Mahwah, NJ: LEA.

Peters, M., Marshall, J. and Fitzsimmons, P. (2000) Managerialism and educational policy in a global context: Foucault, neoliberalism and the doctrine of self-management, in N. Burbules and C.A. Torres (eds) *Globalization and Education, Critical Perspectives*. New York: Routledge.

Power, S. (1992) Researching the impact of education policy: difficulties and discontinuities, *Journal of Education Policy*, 7(5): 493–500.

Prosser, T. (1981) The politics of discretion: aspects of discretionary power in the supplementary benefits scheme, in M. Adler and S. Asquith (eds) *Discretion and Welfare*. London: Heinemann.

Prunty, J. (1985) Signposts for a critical educational policy analysis, *Australian Journal of Education*, 29(2): 133–40.

Ramsey, G. (2000) Quality matters, revitalising teaching: critical times, critical choices, *Report of the Review of Teacher Education*. New South Wales: AGPS.

Ranson, S. (1997) For citizenship and the remaking of civil society, in R. Pring and G. Walford (eds) *Affirming the Comprehensive Ideal*. London: Falmer Press.

Ranson, S. and Stewart, J. (1994) *Management for the Public Domain: Enabling the Learning Society*. New York: St Martin's Press.

Reese, W. (1988) Public schools and the common good, *Educational Theory*, 38: 431–40.

Reich, R. (1991) Secession of the successful, *The New York Times Magazine* (January 20): 42.

Riseborough, G. (1992) Primary headship, state policy and the challenge of the 1990s, *Journal of Education Policy*, 8(2): 123–42.

Rizvi, F. (1997) Educational leadership and the politics of difference, *Melbourne Studies in Education*, 38(1): 91–102.

Rizvi, F. and Kemmis, S. (1987) *Dilemmas of Reform*. Geelong: Deakin University Press.

Robertson, S. (1996) Markets and teacher professionalism: a political economy analysis, *Melbourne Studies in Education*, 37: 23–39.

Sachs, J. (2002) *The Activist Teaching Profession*. Buckingham: Open University Press.

Saks, M. (1983) Removing the blinders? A critique of recent contributions to the sociology of professions, *Sociological Review*, 32(1): 1–21.

Sanders, M.G. (ed.) (2000) *Schooling Students Placed at Risk: Research, Policy and Practice in the Education of Poor and Minority Adolescents*. Mahwah, NJ: Lawrence Erlbaum Associates.

Sayer, A. (1995) *Radical Political Economy: A Critique*. Oxford: Blackwell.

Sayers, S. (1992) The human impact of the market, in P. Heelas and P. Morris (eds) *The Values of the Enterprise Culture: The Moral Debate*. London: Routledge.

Shacklock, G. and Smyth, J. (eds) (1998) *Being Reflexive in Critical Educational and Social Research*. London: Falmer Press.

Shipps, D. (2000) Echoes of corporate influence: managing away urban school troubles, in L. Cuban and D. Shipps (eds) *Reconstructing the Common Good in Education: Coping with Intractable American Dilemmas*. Stanford, CA: Stanford University Press.

Shor, I. and Freire, P. (1987) *A Pedagogy for Liberation: Dialogues on Transforming Education*. Massachusetts: Bergin & Garvey.

Simper, E. (1994) Superhighway may be the wrong route, *The Weekend Australian*: 60.

Slee, R., Weiner, G. with Tomlinson, S. (eds) (1998) *School Effectiveness for Whom?* London: Falmer Press.

Smyth, J. (ed.) (1993) *A Socially Critical View of the Self-Managing School*. London: Falmer Press.

Sparkes, A. and Bloomer, M. (1993) Teaching cultures and school-based management: towards a collaborative reconstruction, in J. Smyth (ed.) *A Socially Critical Review of the Self-Managing School*. London: Falmer Press.

Stilwell, F. (1993) *Economic Inequality: Who Gets What in Australia*. Sydney: Pluto Press.

Stoll, L. and Myers, K. (eds) (1998) *No Quick Fixes: Perspectives on Schools in Difficulty*. London: Falmer Press.

Strathern, M. (ed.) (2000) *Audit Cultures: Anthropological Studies in Accountability, Ethics and the Academy*. London: Routledge.

Stuart Wells, A. and Serna, I. (1996) The politics of culture: understanding local political resistance to detracking in racially mixed schools, *Harvard Educational Review*, 66: 93–118.

Taylor, P. (1999) *Making Sense of Academic Life: Academics, Universities and Change*. Buckingham: Open University Press.

Taylor, S., Rizvi, F., Lingard, B. and Henry, M. (1997) *Educational Policy and the Politics of Change*. London: Routledge.

Thrupp, M. (1997) How school mix shapes school processes: a comparative study of New Zealand schools, *New Zealand Journal of Educational Studies*, 32(1): 53–82.

Thrupp, M. (1999) *Schools Making a Difference – Let's Be Realistic! School Mix, School Effectiveness and the Social Limits of Reform*. Buckingham: Open University Press.

Trow, M. (1974) Problems in the transition from elite to mass education, in *Policies for Higher Education*. Paris: OECD.

Trowler, P. (1998) *Education Policy: A Policy Sociology Approach*. East Sussex: Gildredge Press.

Troyna, B. and Vincent, C. (1995) The discourse of social justice in education, *Discourse Studies in the Cultural Politics of Education*, 16(2): 149–66.

Tsolidis, G. (2000) Diasporic youth: moving beyond the academic versus the popular in school cultures, in J. McLeod and K. Malone (eds) *Researching Youth*. Hobart: ACYS.

Van Parijs, P. (ed.) (1992) *Arguing for Basic Income: Ethical Foundations for a Radical Reform*. London: Verso.

Volmer, H. and Mills, D. (1966) *Professionalization*. Englewood Cliffs, NJ: Prentice-Hall.

Walford, G. (1994) *Choice and Equity in Education*. London: Cassell.

Walford, G. (1997) Privatization and selection, in R. Pring and G. Walford (eds) *Affirming the Comprehensive Ideal*. London: Falmer Press.

Walker, S. and Barton, L. (1989) *Politics and the Processes of Schooling*. Milton Keynes: Open University Press.

Waslander, S. and Thrupp, M. (1995) Choice, competition and segregation: an empirical analysis of a New Zealand secondary school market 1990–1993, *Journal of Education Policy*, 10: 1–26.

Weick, K. (1976) Educational organizations as loosely coupled systems, *Administrative Science Quarterly*, 21: 1–19.

West, C. (1990) The new cultural politics of difference, *October*, 53(summer): 93–109.

White, R.D. (1983) Teachers as state workers and the politics of professionalism. Unpublished PhD, Department of Sociology, Australian National University, Canberra.

Whitty, G., Power, S. and Halpin, D. (1998) *Devolution and Choice in Education: The School, the State and the Market*. Buckingham: Open University Press.

Wilensky, H. (1964) The professionalization of everyone?, *American Journal of Sociology*, 70(2): 137–58.

Wilensky, P. (1986) *Public Power and Public Administration*. Sydney: Hale and Iremonger.

Wilkinson, R.G. (1996) *Unhealthy Societies: The Afflictions of Inequality*. New York: Routledge.

Williams, R. (1961) *The Long Revolution*. London: Chatto and Windus.

Wood, E.M. (1999) *Democracy against Capitalism, Renewing Historical Materialism*. Cambridge: Cambridge University Press.

Yates, L. (2000) Representing 'class' in qualitative research, in J. McLeod and K. Malone (eds) *Researching Youth*. Hobart: ACYS.

Yeatman, A. (1990) *Bureaucrats, Technocrats, Femocrats: Essays on the Contemporary Australian State*. Sydney: Allen & Unwin.

Yeatman, A. (1998a) *Activism and the Policy Process*. Sydney: Allen & Unwin.

Yeatman, A. (1998b) Trends and opportunities in the public sector: a critical assessment, *Australian Journal of Public Administration*, 57(4): 138–47.

Young, I.M. (1990) *Justice and the Politics of Difference*. Princeton, NJ: Princeton University Press.

Index

openup

ideas and understanding
in social science

www.**openup**.co.uk

 **Browse, search and
order online**

 **Download detailed
title information and
sample chapters***

*for selected titles

www.**openup**.co.uk